Praise for *Hope*

MW00655250

An excellent guide to help you pray for your marriage! In the same manner as Beth Moore's *Praying God's Word*, *Hope for Your Marriage: 31 War Room Prayers* will equip you to fight for your marriage. A how-to book that will give you hope and confidence as you ask God to do what He already wants to do for your marriage. I will recommend it to many of my clients!

> ~Gil Martin, Counselor/Smalley Marriage Coach

Jennifer has written a book that will powerfully transform any marriage - whether in the midst of struggle or the mundane day-to-day. Full of Scriptural truth and guided prayers for your husband and your heart, this is a must read to restore (or keep!) hope in your marriage.

> ~Phylicia Masonheimer, Blogger/Author of the book *Christian Cosmo*

As a marriage counselor I have seen couples struggle with every issue including addiction, infidelity and abuse. Whether a couple was floundering because of selfishness or unfaithfulness the key to those who successfully withstood the battle for their marriage were those who had learned dependence on God for wisdom, guidance and instruction. Jennifer White has crafted an amazing tool that will build up your faith and trust in The Lord to guard your heart and to guide your steps. It doesn't matter if your marriage is healthy or hurting, the 31 prayers Jennifer has written will bless you. Each prayer beautifully spoken is also accompanied with appropriate scripture guides and Jennifer's inspired teaching. This book will be a blessing to you and your relationship as you focus on making God the center of your marriage.

> ~Joneal Kirby, PhD, Director of *Heartfelt Ministries*/Author of the book *Heartfelt, A Woman's Guide to Creating Meaningful Friendships*

Do you long to see God do a mighty work in your marriage? Have you ever wanted a friend to show you how to earnestly and effectively pray for your marriage? Jennifer White comes alongside the reader with Scripture, experience and friendship. She draws richly from the Bible to bring about clear guidance for hurting wives, pointing to faith in Christ, and leaving behind fear and bitterness. This powerful book will encourage you to pray for your marriage.

> ~Israel and Brook Wayne, Speakers/Authors/Co-founders of *Family Renewal, LLC.*

Hope for Your Marriage: 31 War Room Prayers gives a practical approach for wives to have a powerful and effective prayer life for her marriage. Jennifer's words will draw you close to the heart of God and your husband. It's an awesome resource for every wife!

> ~Jolene Engle, Author of the book *Wives of the Bible*/Blogger at *JoleneEngle.com*

Hope for your Marriage delivers on its promise, giving words to the prayerful hopes and dreams of committed -- though weary -- wives. Jennifer provides peaceful meditations and convicting challenges that will strengthen hearts and homes for years to come.

> ~Lea Ann Garfias, Author of the book *Rocking Ordinary*

For a Christian wife, fervent prayer is the most powerful thing she can do for her marriage, her husband, and herself. We all need God's power at work in our lives and in our marriages to bring healing and strength. But sometimes it can be difficult for women to know what to pray and exactly how to pray in an effective, productive way. Jennifer makes intimate, meaningful prayer with the Lord a bit easier by providing 31 model prayers about essential spiritual topics for wives. The book is packed with scripture to back up each prayer, which gives even more power to prayer as women absorb the truth of the Word of God into their hearts and minds. I love the simple, concise format. A wife can read a prayer and the related verses each day, and then there is a fantastic personal application where she can write out her own personalized prayer and thoughts. I believe women will get the most out of this book if they do participate by writing their own prayers, as well. This is the kind of book that I believe women will want to go through over and over again as they learn to pray more effectively. I would highly recommend this book to any believing Christian wife.

~April Cassidy, Author of the book *The Peaceful Wife: Living in Submission to Christ as Lord*

If you've ever searched for ways to express God's words of hope and faith over the real issues of your marriage and felt like you're wandering without confident direction, *Hope for Your Marriage: 31 War Room Prayers* is a guidebook for you. Jennifer has crafted prayers that are simple, powerful, well organized and based firmly on God's Word-- prayers that feel authentic and easy to say, not just read. These prayers, the scriptures, and the practical exercises included in each chapter will train the reader in effective spiritual warfare for her marriage. As prayer partners with Jennifer for several years, we have witnessed the intimacy of Jennifer's relationship with our Savior and we've been the grateful recipients of her prayers. These prayers will draw you closer to our Lord and help you to walk in the perpetual victory parade God has designed for your life!

~Robert and Rebecca LeCompte, Founders of *VictoryParade.life*

Hope For Your Marriage is a not just a wonderful tool to help wives pray for their husbands, it is a weapon to fight the enemy of our marriages. Jennifer is aware that Satan is out to kill, steal, and destroy couples, and this book equips us to engage in the spiritual battle for our homes. The 31 themes are applicable to every marriage, and the way she presents each theme leaves the reader ready to wage war. This is a must read for every Bible-believer!

~ Darby Dugger, Speaker/Author/Founder of the Christian website, *DarbyDugger.com*

Hope for Your Marriage

31 War Room Prayers

Jennifer O. White

Dedication

It is my delight to dedicate this book to Dianne, the counselor who introduced me to the power of praying and living in agreement with God's Word. Dianne has led me in hundreds of prayers and helped me experience the power of Jesus' presence and love. Her partnership with the Wonderful Counselor and her leadership in my life are priceless treasures.

Contents

Fight for Freedom from Strongholds

Note to the Reader

I am filled with so much hope for you! Choosing to pray for your marriage is a courageous decision. Doubts may be swirling around that tiny mustard seed of faith you are holding so tightly today. Yet, you have chosen to place your desperate heart in the hands of the One who restores.

Prayer brings you near to the One who is able to open blind eyes and transform the worst offenders into disciple makers. Your prayers can release your pain and the brokenness of your marriage to the One who has unstoppable love to comfort you, unmatched power to heal and stabilize you, and unlimited resources to equip you.

You are making one of life's wisest choices when you pray. You are surrendering Your heart and marriage to the authority of God by allowing His Word to guide your prayers. The Bible is magnificently alive and holds the power to reveal, heal, and deliver husbands and wives.

Ruthless evil forces are at war with you and your husband, but they are no match for God. As you believe, pray, and obey the Word of God, you will be hiding yourself in His strength. You will be aligning yourself with His victorious ways. He will fight for you. He will help you fight your own selfish nature, your impatience, and your attempts to control the situation.

This book is a prayer guide and a battle plan designed to help you rely on God and pursue His best for your marriage. You will find 31 chapters with a prayer, a declaration of faith, Scripture references, and an exercise to help you continue pursuing God on the subject.

Each prayer is written like a psalm to help you express your feelings and agree with the promises of God. If the wording of the prayer does not fit your exact circumstances, let the ideas presented inspire your next conversation with God on the topic.

The declarations of faith you find in each chapter are simple, scriptural summaries. These are battle cries calling your spirit to rise up in agreement with God's Word.

I've listed the Scriptures in the order I refer to them within the preceding prayer. Knowing and believing these truths are critical in your battle plan. Resist the urge to skip over them and rush to the next prayer. Read each verse aloud, look them up, and read them in context. These truths are alive. They are powerful weapons in your spiritual battle. They can slice away the slime of sin. They can heal and deliver you and your husband from evil (Hebrews 4:12; Psalm 107:20).

Each chapter concludes with an opportunity for you to move deeper into the conversation with God. Take your time with these exercises and allow the Holy Spirit to bring more understanding to you. If you need more room to write your answers, use a separate journal. I offer printable journal pages for this book at jenniferowhite.com/shop.

At some point, you may question if your heart is really engaged when you pray words written by someone else. This is one of those sneaky questions the enemy uses to stop people from praying. Here is how I answer the question and avoid the trap: "With my will, I am surrendering these areas of my life to Almighty God. The Word of God is transforming my heart. In the future, my heart will agree with every word and my own prayers will flow easily from within me."

I have written this book for you because I know very personally that connecting with God through prayer is your best hope. If you'd like to learn more about my fight for my marriage, you can read about it in *Prayers for New Brides: Putting on God's Armor After the Wedding Dress.*

I am honored to lead you in prayer for your marriage. I wholeheartedly believe every moment you spend in prayer and Bible study leads you deeper into the rich and satisfying life Christ purchased for you. My mission is to help you see how God's Word applies to your relationship with your husband and help you trust Him with all your needs. May God increase your faith and hope while He equips you in this quest for lasting breakthrough.

Guard yourself against disappointment. God moves on His own timetable. In His Word, we see that He is able to change things suddenly. He also prepares us for trials, afflictions, and waiting. With humility, we ask and keep on asking. We believe and keep on believing. We hope. We pray. We fall and we get back up again. We exercise our faith. We trust God to pursue us every day of our lives with His goodness and mercy.

Lift your head, friend. Seize the confident hope God offers you. Be patient in this trial and constant in prayer (Romans 12:12).

Jennifer O. White
jenniferowhite.com

P.S. Would you be willing to write a short review of this book on Amazon.com? Your honest opinion will help other praying wives in their quest for help and hope.

INTRODUCTION: ANCHORED IN HOPE

"So God has given both his promise and his oath. These two things are unchangeable because it is impossible for God to lie. Therefore, we who have fled to him for refuge can have great confidence as we hold to the hope that lies before us. This hope is a strong and trustworthy anchor for our souls. It leads us through the curtain into God's inner sanctuary."
Hebrews 6:18-19

Jesus purchased hope for us. With His death and resurrection, He made a way for us to be in God's favor. He secured a place for us at God's throne where we can declare our need and receive His help.

Heaven has all that we need.

The burden of what is missing in your marriage may be weighing heavy on you today. Let your faith rise up. Placing your confidence in God comes with a remarkable promise that you will not lack any good thing (Psalm 34:10). Each time you choose to rely on God, you open the door to receive from Him.

You may lack love in your marriage today, but God is offering you His perfect love. You may ache from a lack of faithfulness in your marriage, but God has always been and always will be faithful to you. The best thing that can come out of your difficult days of marriage is a bold assurance that God is everything you will ever need.

Each time God answers one of your prayers, let it be a reminder to you that He is in charge. He is worthy of our deepest devotion. He is exceedingly generous.

While you wait for Him to answer your prayers, His Word will be your anchor. Let it fuel your hope with evidence that He is good, He is able, He is magnificent.

While so many things are impossible for husbands and wives, nothing is impossible for our God. Marriage problems wake us up to our weaknesses and the frailty of our human nature. Thankfully a relationship with God is founded on the fact that we are weak and He is strong. In 2 Corinthians 12:9-10, God invites us to be completely upfront with Him about our weaknesses. In return, He promises to bring His power to rest on us in that very area of difficulty. Every shortcoming you and your husband bring to your marriage can be overcome when placed in the capable hands of Jesus.

SECTION 1: FIGHT FROM A PLACE OF VICTORY

Jesus secured for you a victorious life. He conquered the power of sin and death. Instead of being overwhelmed by the effects of sin, you can live an overcoming life. Your husband can too.

The enemy of your marriage wants you to think powerless, hopeless thoughts. Your battle is to see through these lies. You are standing on much higher ground. You are walking in Jesus' perpetual victory parade as a trophy of His grace.

If your husband has not accepted Jesus as Lord of his life, the second prayer will guide you in bringing his greatest need to God. May God give you great boldness and perseverance as you pray.

In the Messiah, in Christ, God leads us from place to place in one perpetual victory parade. Through us, he brings knowledge of Christ.
2 Corinthians 2:14 MSG

I have told you all this so that you may have peace in me. Here on earth you will have many trials and sorrows. But take heart, because I have overcome the world.
John 16:33

No, despite all these things, overwhelming victory is ours through Christ, who loved us.

Romans 8:37

CHAPTER 1

MORE THAN A CONQUEROR

Oh God, help us! I feel so defeated by the constant barrage of problems and setbacks in our marriage. Evil is infecting our household. I'm mentally, emotionally, and physically exhausted.

My soul needs rest. I'm desperate for those green pastures and still waters You have promised. But how can I possibly rest when my most important earthly relationship is in critical condition?

Open my spiritual eyes. I want to see the reality of Jesus triumphing over this present darkness.

Your Word says Jesus conquered sin and the death it brings. I call on the resurrection power of Jesus to help us resist our sinful natures. Teach us both to cooperate with the life-giving power of Your Holy Spirit. Breathe Your life into our sacred union.

You are our only hope. Hide us away from the evil one in the shelter of Your wings. I place my faith in You as the One who shields us from Satan's evil schemes. Thank You for sending Jesus to conquer the works of the devil.

Amen

Declaration of Faith

Jesus is more powerful than anything that comes against us.

Scripture References

He makes me lie down in green pastures. He leads me beside still waters. Psalm 23:2 ESV

But thank God! He gives us victory over sin and death through our Lord Jesus Christ. 1 Corinthians 15:57

No, despite all these things, overwhelming victory is ours through Christ, who loved us. Romans 8:37

And because you belong to him, the power of the life-giving Spirit has freed you from the power of sin that leads to death. Romans 8:2

Then he said to me, "Speak a prophetic message to the winds, son of man. Speak a prophetic message and say, 'This is what the Sovereign LORD says: Come, O breath, from the four winds! Breathe into these dead bodies so they may live again.'" Ezekiel 37:9

He will cover you with his feathers. He will shelter you with his wings. His faithful promises are your armor and protection. Psalm 91:4

The LORD is my strength and shield. I trust him with all my heart. He helps me, and my heart is filled with joy. I burst out in songs of thanksgiving. Psalm 28:7

For every child of God defeats this evil world, and we achieve this victory through our faith. 1 John 5:4

But when people keep on sinning, it shows that they belong to the devil, who has been sinning since the beginning. But the Son of God came to destroy the works of the devil. 1 John 3:8

But in that coming day no weapon turned against you will succeed. You will silence every voice raised up to accuse you. These benefits are enjoyed by the servants of the LORD; their vindication will come from me. I, the LORD, have spoken! Isaiah 54:17

Make it Personal

Using Psalm 28:7 as a guide, write your own short prayer of thanksgiving.

_____

_____

_____

_____

_____

_____

So the LORD must wait for
you to come to him so he
can show you his love and
compassion. For the LORD
is a faithful God. Blessed are
those who wait for his help.

Isaiah 30:18

CHAPTER 2

HIS SALVATION

If your husband has not chosen Jesus as his Savior, this prayer can guide you in praying for him.

God, I come asking for mercy for my husband. He is a sinner who has not yet acknowledged Your place of authority in his life. He has not been able to relinquish his own way of life for Yours. He does not realize the life he has chosen leads to poverty and hunger here on earth, in our marriage, and after his natural life.

You have already done so much for him. You sent Jesus to die for his sins and rescue him from a life separated from Your goodness. I am asking You for more. I am asking You to intervene again and again. Only You have the power to awaken him to what is missing in his life. I choose a life of praying for him knowing that You will use it as a weapon to destroy every false belief that keeps him from knowing You.

I trust Your creative power to reach him. I invite You to use dreams, visions, and even things like burning bushes to reveal Yourself to him. I humbly accept my role in attracting him to You. With the help of Your

Spirit, I will not nag or preach at him. Instead, I will die to myself and allow the life of Christ within me to draw him to You.

Thank You, God, for Your great love for him. Thank You for enduring his lack of repentance and waiting patiently for him to repent. Help me to do the same.

Amen

Declaration of Faith

God is patiently waiting for my husband to repent and empowering me to do the same.

Scripture References

The godly eat to their hearts' content, but the belly of the wicked goes hungry. Proverbs 13:25

Even strong young lions sometimes go hungry, but those who trust in the LORD will lack no good thing. Psalm 34:10

For God presented Jesus as the sacrifice for sin. People are made right with God when they believe that Jesus sacrificed his life, shedding his blood. This sacrifice shows that God was being fair when he held back and did not punish those who sinned in times past, Romans 3:25

Jesus gave his life for our sins, just as God our Father planned, in order to rescue us from this evil world in which we live. Galatians 1:4

Yes, I am sending you to the Gentiles to open their eyes, so they may turn from darkness to light and from the power of Satan to God. Then they will receive forgiveness for their sins and be given a place among God's people, who are set apart by faith in me. Acts 26:17b-18

We use God's mighty weapons, not worldly weapons, to knock down the strongholds of human reasoning and to destroy false arguments. We destroy every proud obstacle that keeps people from knowing God. We capture their rebellious thoughts and teach them to obey Christ.
2 Corinthians 10:5

He speaks in dreams, in visions of the night, when deep sleep falls on people as they lie in their beds. Job 33:15

In the same way, you wives must accept the authority of your husbands. Then, even if some refuse to obey the Good News, your godly lives will speak to them without any words. They will be won over by observing your pure and reverent lives. 1 Peter 3:1-2

Love is patient and kind. Love never gives up, never loses faith, is always hopeful, and endures through every circumstance. 1 Corinthians 13:4a,7

The Lord isn't really being slow about his promise, as some people think. No, he is being patient for your sake. He does not want anyone to be destroyed, but wants everyone to repent. 2 Peter 3:9

Make it Personal

Rewrite 1 Peter 3:1-2 in your own words. Write it as a declaration and personalize it using your names.

_____

_____

_____

_____

_____

_____

SECTION 2: FIGHT FOR WHAT WILL LAST

We live in a society that values disposable things. People are in the habit of throwing things and even people away. Spouses are rejected. Vows are broken. Children of divorce often find themselves repeating the cycle even when they are desperate for the stability of lasting love.

God offers a very different way of life. In His Kingdom, promises are fulfilled. He remains faithful even when His people lose their way. Membership in the family of God is a secure place. Prodigals can come home. Betrayals, along with all other sins, are forgiven. The weak and the wounded have a place at God's family dinner table.

God established the marriage between husband and wife to reflect the covenant Christ made with His Bridegroom, the Church (Ephesians 5:32). This abiding love of Christ is deeply implanted in His followers. The Holy Spirit empowers His people to reject the world's ideas and embrace God's faithful ways.

We all have earthly possessions that we treasure, but The Bible tells us not to store up treasures on earth that are temporary. It tells us to store up heavenly treasures (Matthew 6:19-21). The prayers in this section will help you choose treasures for yourself and your husband that will endure this life on earth and long after your last breath.

I will confirm my covenant with you and your descendants after you,
from generation to generation. This is the everlasting covenant:
I will always be your God and the God of your descendants after you.
Genesis 17:7

Give honor to
marriage, and
remain faithful
to one another
in marriage.

Hebrews 13:4a

CHAPTER 3

MARRIAGE

Consider this, friend; marriage was designed by God to be honored and enjoyed until we leave this earth. It is an earthly treasure reminding us of our heavenly marriage to Jesus, our Bridegroom. It is a ministry of enduring faithfulness and service.

God, I know You are the Creator of marriage and You require us to honor it. I confess that I have not honored our marriage with my words and actions. Please forgive me.

You are honoring Your commitment to me without fail. You respond to my imperfections with relentless mercy and goodness. I want to serve my husband with the same compassion You have for me.

Help me to be steadfast in keeping my vows and help my spouse to do the same.

Please forgive both of us where we have been unfaithful. Create in us clean and merciful hearts.

Bless us with Godly marriage mentors and help us to be teachable. I believe You are able to cause our marriage to thrive. My hope is we will one day be mentors helping other couples honor Your way and Your idea of marriage.

Amen

Declaration of Faith

I honor God's faithfulness to me by remaining faithful to
my marriage vows.

Scripture References

Give honor to marriage, and remain faithful to one another in marriage. God will surely judge people who are immoral and those who commit adultery. Hebrews 13:4

Surely your goodness and unfailing love will pursue me all the days of my life, and I will live in the house of the LORD forever. Psalm 23:6

Oh, that my ways were steadfast in obeying your decrees!
Psalm 119:5 NIV

Create in me a clean heart, O God. Renew a loyal spirit within me.
Psalm 51:10

Truly God is good to Israel, to those whose hearts are pure. Psalm 73:1

As iron sharpens iron, so a friend sharpens a friend. Proverbs 27:17

Make it Personal

Take a moment to forgive those who have modeled unfaithfulness in marriage to you. Invite God to forgive them and to equip you with His strength to live differently.

_____

_____

_____

_____

_____

_____

Three things will
last forever—faith,
hope, and love—
and the greatest
of these is love.

1 Corinthians 13:13

CHAPTER 4

FAITH

God, Your Word says that nothing is impossible for You. I know You are pleased when I believe in You. Restoring our marriage feels impossible to me, but I choose to believe it is certainly within Your power.

I confess to You my sin of not relying on You for all we need. Please forgive me and grant me greater humility that equips me to pray about everything.

Increase my faith, God. Help me to look to You for the help we need instead of despairing over what has been said and done between us.

I choose to believe that Jesus' covenant with me has given me access to every spiritual blessing including Your mighty power to restore what has been broken in our hearts and our marriage.

Amen

Declaration of Faith

My faith in God's power to heal this marriage is increasing.

Scripture References

Jesus looked at them intently and said, 'Humanly speaking, it is impossible. But with God everything is possible. Matthew 19:26

And it is impossible to please God without faith. Anyone who wants to come to Him must believe that God exists and that He rewards those who sincerely seek him. Hebrews 11:6

Never stop praying. 1 Thessalonians 5:17

The father instantly cried out, "I do believe, but help me overcome my unbelief!" Mark 9:24

All praise to God, the Father of our Lord Jesus Christ, who has blessed us with every spiritual blessing in the heavenly realms because we are united with Christ. Ephesians 1:3

When Job prayed for his friends, the LORD restored his fortunes. In fact, the LORD gave him twice as much as before! Job 42:11

Make it Personal

Write out what you believe God can do in your marriage. This is not you telling Him what to do. This is simply an act of worshipping Him as the One who is able to do it.

_____

_____

_____

_____

_____

_____

I pray that God, the
source of hope, will fill
you completely with joy
and peace because you
trust in him. Then you will
overflow with confident
hope through the power
of the Holy Spirit.

Romans 15:13

CHAPTER 5

HOPE

Without You, God, our marriage has no hope. Strengthen my weary heart so that I put my hope for our marriage in Your unfailing love and power. I choose to believe that I will never be disappointed if I focus on Your faithfulness to me.

Sarah, Elizabeth and Hannah were childless, but You fulfilled their dreams and prayers. They waited longer than anyone expected they should. I choose to trust that You are able to bring new life into our marriage. I will wait expectantly, and I will worship You while I wait.

Help me Lord not to be discouraged and weakened by the "it's time to give up" messages others speak over our marriage. Strengthen me to stand firm on Your promises.

David was just a shepherd boy, but he chose to fight Goliath. He charged ahead remembering the victory You gave him over the lion and the bear. God, I need You to remind me how You have helped me in the past. Let my hope be as secure as David's.

I choose to trust that You really do have a good plan for my life and my husband. Your Word says that You reward faith, and I believe You will reward mine.

Amen

Declaration of Faith

My hope is anchored in the promise of God's good plan for our marriage.

Scripture References

And so, Lord, where do I put my hope? My only hope is in you.
Psalm 39:7

But I will keep on hoping for your help; I will praise you more and more.
Psalm 71:14

But if we look forward to something we don't yet have, we must wait patiently and confidently. Romans 8:25

Stand your ground, putting on the belt of truth and the body armor of God's righteousness. Ephesians 6:14

I pray that God, the source of hope, will fill you completely with joy and peace because you trust in him. Then you will overflow with confident hope through the power of the Holy Spirit. Romans 15:13

For I know the plans I have for you, says the LORD. They are plans for good and not for disaster, to give you a future and a hope.
Jeremiah 29:11

You will be rewarded for this; your hope will not be disappointed.
Proverbs 23:18

Make it Personal

Have you lost hope in the past and reacted hastily causing even deeper wounds in your marriage? Confess this to God below and ask for His forgiveness and restoration.

_____

_____

_____

_____

_____

_____

_____

We love each
other because
he loved us first.

———————▼———————

1 John 4:19

CHAPTER 6

LOVE

God, Your promise to me is unfailing love. I need it now more than ever. Many unloving things have been said and done in this marriage. I am grateful that Your love for me and my spouse never fails.

Increase my awareness of Your love, God. Help me to see You as gentle and kind toward me. Help me to trust You as my Sustainer, the One who satisfies my weary soul.

Let Your perfect love drive away the fears of rejection and loneliness. Let it be a bright, warm, and unceasing flame guiding us.

Fuel our love for each other, God. By Your power, our marriage will be a beautiful reflection of Your covenant with the Bride of Christ.

Amen

Declaration of Faith

I receive God's faithful love and it drives away my fear.

Scripture References

Give thanks to the Lord, for he is good! His faithful love endures forever.
Psalm 136:1

But the Holy Spirit produces this kind of fruit in our lives: love, joy, peace, patience, kindness, goodness, faithfulness, gentleness, and self-control. There is no law against these things! Galatians 5:22-23

Love is patient and kind. Love is not jealous or boastful or proud.
1 Corinthians 13:4

Surely God is my help; the Lord is the one who sustains me.
Psalm 54:4 NIV

He gives power to the weak and strength to the powerless. Isaiah 40:29

Such love has no fear, because perfect love expels all fear. If we are afraid, it is for fear of punishment, and this shows that we have not fully experienced his perfect love. 1 John 4:18

Love never gives up, never loses faith, is always hopeful, and endures through every circumstance. 1 Corinthians 13:7

Make it Personal

In 1 John 4:18, we learn that God's perfect love expels fear. What are your fears? List them below in a prayer of confession to God. Invite Him to help you overcome those fears by revealing His perfect love.

_____

_____

_____

_____

_____

Whatever is good and perfect comes down to us from God our Father, who created all the lights in the heavens. He never changes or casts a shifting shadow.

James 1:17

SECTION 3: FIGHT FOR YOUR GOOD GIFTS

God is a generous giver! He gives us new life in Christ. He shares with us all the spiritual blessings of heaven. In John 10:10, He promises to triumph over Satan's plan to kill, steal and destroy. He ensures us that life in Christ will be rich and satisfying.

Choosing God's way to contentment requires a fight. Get ready to wrestle your own expectations to the ground. Get ready to nurture the life of Christ within you and become a new wife to your husband.

With the following prayers, you are inviting God to equip you to be victorious in marriage.

*So if you sinful people know how to give good gifts
to your children, how much more will your heavenly
Father give good gifts to those who ask him.*
Matthew 7:11

*From his abundance we have all received one
gracious blessing after another.*
John 1:16

In that day he will be your
sure foundation, providing
a rich store of salvation,
wisdom, and knowledge.
The fear of the LORD
will be your treasure.

———————▼———————

Isaiah 33:6

CHAPTER 7

STABILITY AND STRENGTH

Oh God, our marriage feels so unstable. Harsh words, threats, and betrayals have me questioning our future together.

I expected marriage to be the best part of my life. I expected it to be the place where I could feel safe, cherished, and whole. Where did we go wrong? Show me the ways I need to change. Help me take responsibility for my attitude and actions in our marriage. Help my husband do the same.

My thoughts and emotions often spiral into self-pity. "What ifs" and worst-case scenarios overwhelm me. I react with anger and defensiveness when my spouse is unhappy and unkind. I am looking up to You now, Lord. You are the One who establishes my worth. Your love for me is unending. You are the One who sets my feet on solid ground. You are for me, so what can any human do to diminish me? You chose me. You are the source of my safety and wholeness.

Your Word says those who listen to Your teaching and follow it build their house on a solid foundation. Where have we ignored Your teaching, God? Please open our eyes to see our sin. Help us choose Your way so these trials and those to come will not destroy us.

You are the Creator and Sustainer of the universe. Surely, holding our marriage together is not too hard for You. I am looking to You now as the Savior of this marriage. I am boldly coming to Your throne asking for the stability and strength You offer us.

You are always with me to help me. Help me rely on You more, God. I want to have a continual dialogue with You about every issue that arises. I trust that Your Holy Spirit will impart the wisdom I need moment by moment, so I can respond to issues with truth and unfailing love.

Your Word reminds me that Christians should expect to endure trials and heartache. You make it clear that I do not wrestle against my spouse, but against the powers of darkness. I choose to fight the real enemy by standing under Your leadership, armed with Your appointed weapons. I will fight for my marriage and not against it. Thank You for equipping me for this battle.

I will persevere through the trials of this marriage with my mind set on You and doing marriage Your way. I will not fear because You are with me. You are victorious.

I will wait to receive all that You have promised to those who follow You.

Amen

Declaration of Faith

I persevere through every trial expecting God to miraculously sustain me.

Scripture References

He lifted me out of the pit of despair, out of the mud and the mire. He set my feet on solid ground and steadied me as I walked along.
Psalm 40:2

If God is for us, who can ever be against us? Romans 8:31b

Anyone who listens to my teaching and follows it is wise, like a person who builds a house on solid rock. Matthew 7:24

When the storms of life come, the wicked are whirled away, but the godly have a lasting foundation. Proverbs 10:25

Wickedness never brings stability, but the godly have deep roots.
Proverbs 12:3

In that day he will be your sure foundation, providing a rich store of salvation, wisdom, and knowledge. The fear of the Lord will be your treasure. Isaiah 33:6

I know the Lord is always with me. I will not be shaken, for he is right beside me. Psalm 16:8

He alone is my rock and my salvation, my fortress where I will never be shaken. Psalm 62:2

Pray in the Spirit at all times and on every occasion. Stay alert and be persistent in your prayers for all believers everywhere. Ephesians 6:18

... asking God, the glorious Father of our Lord Jesus Christ, to give you spiritual wisdom and insight so that you might grow in your knowledge of God. Ephesians 1:17

Dear friends, don't be surprised at the fiery trials you are going through, as if something strange were happening to you. 1 Peter 4:12

For we are not fighting against flesh-and-blood enemies, but against evil rulers and authorities of the unseen world, against mighty powers in this dark world, and against evil spirits in the heavenly places. Ephesians 6:12

Put on all of God's armor so that you will be able to stand firm against all strategies of the devil. Ephesians 6:11

The LORD is for me, so I will have no fear. What can mere people do to me? Psalm 118:6

Patient endurance is what you need now, so that you will continue to do God's will. Then you will receive all that he has promised. Hebrews 10:36

Make it Personal

Psalm 16:8 says that you "will not be shaken." Write your own prayer below inviting God to make you unshakeable in an area of your life where you feel crushed or unstable.

_____

_____

_____

_____

_____

If you need wisdom, ask our
generous God, and he will give
it to you. He will not rebuke you
for asking. But when you ask
him, be sure that your faith is
in God alone. Do not waver,
for a person with divided
loyalty is as unsettled as a
wave of the sea that is blown
and tossed by the wind.

James 1:5-6

CHAPTER 8

GODLY WISDOM

Oh God! My husband and I need Your wise counsel. In our own wisdom, we've failed each other miserably. Please forgive us for relying on our own insight instead of seeking Your way.

Help us to see how we have opposed Your wisdom by following our hearts. Teach us to follow the leadership of Your Spirit instead of our own desires for perfection, vindication, and control.

I trust Your wisdom will lead to peace, gentleness, and sincerity between us. Oh how we need Your help showing mercy to each other. I trust Your wisdom to help us yield to You and each other instead of demanding our own way.

Make me ready to follow Your leadership. Teach me to recognize Your voice and trust it. Help my husband do the same. Grant us the gift of Your wise counsel through teachers, preachers, counselors, and God-fearing friends.

Thank You, God, for offering us the safety and pleasure of living wisely.

Amen

Declaration of Faith

I place my hope in God's wisdom and leadership.

Scripture References

Those who trust their own insight are foolish, but anyone who walks in wisdom is safe. Proverbs 28:26

I keep asking that the God of our Lord Jesus Christ, the glorious Father, may give you the Spirit of wisdom and revelation, so that you may know him better. I pray that the eyes of your heart may be enlightened in order that you may know the hope to which he has called you, the riches of his glorious inheritance in his holy people, ... Ephesians 1:17-18 NIV

"The human heart is the most deceitful of all things, and desperately wicked. Who really knows how bad it is? Jeremiah 17:9

But the wisdom from above is first of all pure. It is also peace loving, gentle at all times, and willing to yield to others. It is full of mercy and good deeds. It shows no favoritism and is always sincere. James 3:17

My sheep listen to my voice; I know them, and they follow me. John 10:27

Let the message about Christ, in all its richness, fill your lives. Teach and counsel each other with all the wisdom he gives. Sing psalms and hymns and spiritual songs to God with thankful hearts. Colossians 3:16

Doing wrong is fun for a fool, but living wisely brings pleasure to the sensible. Proverbs 10:23

Make it Personal

Using James 3:17 as a guide, confess to God the unwise ways you have interacted with your husband. Then ask for God's wisdom and courage to relate with him differently.

_____

_____

_____

_____

_____

_____

Instead, be kind to each
other, tenderhearted,
forgiving one another,
just as God through
Christ has forgiven you.

———————▼———————

Ephesians 4:32

CHAPTER 9

FORGIVEN

God, my mind is fixed on this seemingly unforgivable issue in our marriage. My heart rages at this betrayal of my trust. My mouth is spewing horrible things about my husband and this marriage. My thoughts are even worse.

Here is my furious and broken heart, Lord. I am handing You the reigns of my mind and this marriage. Only You could sort out this tangled mess of my emotions.

Your love endures. How do You endure my sin against You, Lord? How do You forgive me again and again? I am so weak in this area of forgiveness, but You are strong. Empower me to forgive my husband. Please help him to be forgiving toward me too.

Wonderful Counselor, teach us both to be quick to confess our sins to You and each other. Transform us by the power of Your Word so that we are able to resist the temptation to repeat the same sin in the future. Nothing is impossible for You, God.

Today, I reject the fear that I will be made a fool if I forgive. Jesus chose to forgive those who crucified Him. I choose to follow His example and allow forgiveness to flow from within me like an endless fountain. I will not allow my feelings to keep me from obeying Your command to forgive. I will speak the words of forgiveness, and trust Your Holy Spirit to do the healing work in my heart.

Amen

Declaration of Faith

I choose to forgive and live in obedience to God.

Scripture References

Love never gives up, never loses faith, is always hopeful, and endures through every circumstance. 1 Corinthians 13:7

Praise the LORD! Give thanks to the LORD, for he is good! His faithful love endures forever. Psalm 106:1

He gives power to the weak and strength to the powerless. Isaiah 40:29

But if we confess our sins to him, he is faithful and just to forgive us our sins and to cleanse us from all wickedness. 1 John 1:9

Confess your sins to each other and pray for each other so that you may be healed. The earnest prayer of a righteous person has great power and produces wonderful results. James 5:16

Don't copy the behavior and customs of this world, but let God transform you into a new person by changing the way you think. Then you will learn to know God's will for you, which is good and pleasing and perfect. Romans 12:2

He sent out his word and healed them, snatching them from the door of death. Psalm 107:20

So humble yourselves before God. Resist the devil, and he will flee from you. James 4:6

Jesus looked at them intently and said, "Humanly speaking, it is impossible. But with God everything is possible. Matthew 19:26

Jesus said, "Father, forgive them, for they don't know what they are doing." And the soldiers gambled for his clothes by throwing dice. Luke 23:34

Then Peter came to him and asked, "Lord, how often should I forgive someone who sins against me? Seven times?" "No, not seven times," Jesus replied, "but seventy times seven! Matthew 18:21-22

But when you are praying, first forgive anyone you are holding a grudge against, so that your Father in heaven will forgive your sins, too." Mark 11:25

Make it Personal

List at least one thing you have repeatedly needed God's forgiveness for. Thank Him for His commitment to forgive you every single time. Invite Him to fan the flame of His forgiving Spirit in your heart toward your husband.

_____

_____

_____

_____

_____

_____

_____

_____

_____

Always be humble and
gentle. Be patient with
each other, making
allowance for each
other's faults because
of your love.

———————▼———————

Ephesians 4:2

CHAPTER 10

GENTLENESS

God, I have not always thought of You as gentle. I am guilty of comparing You to humans that are often harsh in their leadership. Please teach me about Your gentleness toward me. Help me to feel safe with You.

My words and actions toward my husband have not been gentle. Forgive me, Father. I want to be different, but I don't know how.

Help me not to stir up anger in my spouse with arguments. Show me how to communicate in a way that soothes and opens the door for healthy responses.

I want to honor You by speaking the truth in love. Take this bitterness, contempt, and resentment from me, Lord. Enable me to speak without snarling. Please send me someone to model this for me.

I choose to cooperate with Your Holy Spirit who will nurture the unfading beauty of a gentle and quiet spirit within me. You make all things new, and I look forward to being brand new in this area, God. Please help my husband recognize Your gentleness toward him and learn to treat me the same way.

Amen

Declaration of Faith

God has chosen to be gentle to me. He enables me to be gentle toward my spouse.

Scripture References

Take my yoke upon you. Let me teach you, because I am humble and gentle at heart, and you will find rest for your souls. Matthew 11:29

"Go out and stand before me on the mountain," the LORD told him. And as Elijah stood there, the LORD passed by, and a mighty windstorm hit the mountain. It was such a terrible blast that the rocks were torn loose, but the LORD was not in the wind. After the wind there was an earthquake, but the LORD was not in the earthquake. And after the earthquake there was a fire, but the LORD was not in the fire. And after the fire there was the sound of a gentle whisper. 1 Kings 19:11-12

A gentle answer deflects anger, but harsh words make tempers flare. Proverbs 15:1

They must not slander anyone and must avoid quarreling. Instead, they should be gentle and show true humility to everyone. Titus 3:2

Instead, we will speak the truth in love, growing in every way more and more like Christ, who is the head of his body, the church. Ephesians 4:15

You should clothe yourselves instead with the beauty that comes from within, the unfading beauty of a gentle and quiet spirit, which is so precious to God. 1 Peter 3:4

But the fruit of the Spirit is love, joy, peace, patience, kindness, goodness, faithfulness, gentleness, self-control; against such things there is no law. Galatians 5:22-23

Make it Personal

Write your own prayer and declaration of faith using Titus 3:2 as a guide.

_____

_____

_____

_____

_____

_____

Don't be selfish; don't
try to impress others.
Be humble, thinking
of others as better
than yourselves.

—————▼—————

Philippians 2:3

CHAPTER 11

HUMILITY

God, I confess that I often attempt to fix our marriage without waiting on You for wisdom. You have allowed me to see how powerless I am to make any lasting changes on my own. Please forgive me for this lack of humble dependence on You.

Today, I am declaring that Your way to think is the best way. I humbly surrender my preconceived ideas about being a wife and about marriage.

Give me eyes to see the humility of Christ, and how it relates to my relationship with my husband. Let Christ's humility be the foundation for my thoughts, words, and actions.

Make me brand new for the sake of the one I have pledged to love faithfully.

Train me to ask You for help, God. I want to excel at bringing my weaknesses to You and asking for Your promised gift of strength in those areas.

Your Word says that humility comes before honor. I trust that as I obey You, You will reward me with honor in Your kingdom and especially in this marriage.

Slay my pride, Lord, so it doesn't interfere with my relationship with You or my husband. I invite You to help my husband in the same way.

Amen

Declaration of Faith

I choose the humility of Christ, and I receive the help I need from God.

Scripture References

Jesus told him, "I am the way, the truth, and the life. No one can come to the Father except through me. John 14:6

For, "Who can know the LORD's thoughts? Who knows enough to teach him?" But we understand these things, for we have the mind of Christ. 1 Corinthians 2:16

This means that anyone who belongs to Christ has become a new person. The old life is gone; a new life has begun! 2 Corinthians 5:17

So let us come boldly to the throne of our gracious God. There we will receive his mercy, and we will find grace to help us when we need it most. Hebrews 4:16

Each time he said, "My grace is all you need. My power works best in weakness." So now I am glad to boast about my weaknesses, so that the power of Christ can work through me. 2 Corinthians 12:9

Proud people will be ruined, but the humble will be honored. Proverbs 18:22 NCV

True humility and fear of the LORD lead to riches, honor, and long life. Proverbs 22:4

Fear of the LORD teaches wisdom; humility precedes honor. Proverbs 15:33

And all of you, serve each other in humility, for "God opposes the proud but favors the humble." 1 Peter 5:5b

Make it Personal

One of the ways you can serve your husband in humility is by praying for him. Use two of the above Scriptures to guide you in writing a prayer for him.

_____

_____

_____

_____

_____

_____

Those who know your name trust in you, for you, O LORD, do not abandon those who search for you.

Psalm 9:10

CHAPTER 12

TRUST

God, how can I continue to live in a marriage where there is no trust? How did we get here? It seems like we have broken every promise we made to each other.

I may not trust my husband right now, but I know that I can trust Your unfailing love for both of us. Thank You for being my rock. I put our broken marriage in Your hands.

I confess to You that I have not been trustworthy. Please forgive me, God, and help my spouse forgive me. Create in me a wholehearted desire to be truthful, honorable and responsible. Let Your resurrection power strengthen me in these areas of overwhelming weakness. Please do the same for my spouse.

I choose to forgive him for every lie and broken promise because You have chosen to do the same for me, God. Trust is earned slowly, and I will wait for this to happen between us. I will rely on You for the patience and perseverance I need.

You are able to make all things new. I choose to believe we can be transformed. Please remake us in Your image. Renew our minds so our marriage is fertile ground for honesty and reliability.

Amen

Declaration of Faith

God empowers me to keep my word, especially my vows.

Scripture References

But when I am afraid, I will put my trust in you. Psalm 56:3

But I trust in your unfailing love. I will rejoice because you have rescued me. Psalm 13:5

Commit everything you do to the LORD. Trust him, and he will help you. Psalm 37:5

But if we confess our sins to him, he is faithful and just to forgive us our sins and to cleanse us from all wickedness. 1 John 1:9

The Spirit of God, who raised Jesus from the dead, lives in you. And just as God raised Christ Jesus from the dead, he will give life to your mortal bodies by this same Spirit living within you. Romans 8:11

Each time he said, "My grace is all you need. My power works best in weakness." So now I am glad to boast about my weaknesses, so that the power of Christ can work through me. 2 Corinthians 12:9

If you forgive those who sin against you, your heavenly Father will forgive you. Matthew 6:14

May God, who gives this patience and encouragement, help you live in complete harmony with each other, as is fitting for followers of Christ Jesus. Romans 15:5

Patient endurance is what you need now, so that you will continue to do God's will. Then you will receive all that he has promised. Hebrews 10:36

For I am about to do something new. See, I have already begun! Do you not see it? I will make a pathway through the wilderness. I will create rivers in the dry wasteland. Isaiah 43:19

Don't copy the behavior and customs of this world, but let God transform you into a new person by changing the way you think. Then you will learn to know God's will for you, which is good and pleasing and perfect. Romans 12:2

Make it Personal

Have you broken vows you made to God and your husband? Use the space below to confess them to God and ask for His forgiveness. Seek forgiveness from your husband as well. Invite the Holy Spirit to direct your words and prepare your husband for the interaction.

And this righteousness
will bring peace. Yes, it
will bring quietness and
confidence forever.

Isaiah 32:17

CHAPTER 13

PEACE

God, some days my heart and our home feel chaotic, even warlike. Our words often sound like missiles launched at each other. I long for Your promise of perfect peace to be a reality in our marriage.

I believe that Jesus is the Prince of Peace who has created peace between You and me. Thank You for this indescribable gift! I confess I have failed at following Your instructions and His example of peaceful living. Today, I choose for myself the wellness and wholeness that comes from a life of obedience to You, God. Please help my husband do the same.

Train me to keep my mind focused on You. When I am offended, help me respond quickly with forgiveness. When I am lonely and feel misunderstood, help me to remember that You are with me and know all my thoughts and feelings. When I am angry, help me rely on You for responses that build up and protect our relationship. When I am distraught, help me to find hope in Your promise to bring beauty from the ashes.

I trust You as my Shepherd who leads me away from man-made efforts to establish peace. With Your help, I will not use flattery, manipulation, lies, intimidation and other methods of control to create a false sense of peace between my spouse and me.

I will stand still in the heat of the battle, trusting You to fight for me, and bring Your true peace to our home.

Amen

Declaration of Faith

I keep my thoughts on Jesus who keeps me in perfect peace
regardless of my circumstances.

Scripture References

You will keep in perfect peace all who trust in you, all whose thoughts are fixed on you! Isaiah 26:1

Then you will experience God's peace, which exceeds anything we can understand. His peace will guard your hearts and minds as you live in Christ Jesus. Philippians 4:7

For a child is born to us, a son is given to us. The government will rest on his shoulders. And he will be called: Wonderful Counselor, Mighty God, Everlasting Father, Prince of Peace. Isaiah 9:6

Those who love your instructions have great peace and do not stumble.
Psalm 119:65

And this righteousness will bring peace. Yes, it will bring quietness and confidence forever. Isaiah 32:17

So letting your sinful nature control your mind leads to death. But letting the Spirit control your mind leads to life and peace. Romans 8:6

"Look! The virgin will conceive a child! She will give birth to a son, and they will call him Immanuel, which means 'God is with us.'"
Matthew 1:23

If you forgive those who sin against you, your heavenly Father will forgive you. Matthew 6:14

You know when I sit down or stand up. You know my thoughts even when I'm far away. Psalm 139:2

And "don't sin by letting anger control you." Don't let the sun go down while you are still angry, ... Ephesians 4:26

To all who mourn in Israel, he will give a crown of beauty for ashes, a joyous blessing instead of mourning, festive praise instead of despair. In their righteousness, they will be like great oaks that the LORD has planted for his own glory. Isaiah 61:3

Let us therefore make every effort to do what leads to peace and to mutual edification. Romans 14:19

The LORD is my shepherd; I have all that I need. Psalm 23:1

Such people are not serving Christ our Lord; they are serving their own personal interests. By smooth talk and glowing words they deceive innocent people. Romans 16:18

Don't lie to each other, for you have stripped off your old sinful nature and all its wicked deeds. Colossians 3:9

The LORD himself will fight for you. Just stay calm. Exodus 14:14

Make it Personal

Have you ever tried to keep the peace in your marriage by avoiding confrontation and/or withholding information? Those choices are driven by fear. They conflict with Jesus' truthful way. Write a prayer inviting God to teach you a new way to achieve peace in your relationship with your husband.

_____

_____

_____

_____

_____

_____

Finishing is better
than starting. Patience
is better than pride.

Ecclesiastes 7:8

CHAPTER 14

PATIENCE

Lord, I've been praying for our marriage and nothing appears to be changing. Today, I'm operating from an empty tank. My nerves are fried! How do I endure these lonely, hard days? How long do I hold on? What do I do while I wait for Your changes in me and in him?

You promised Abraham a son. Twenty-five years later, You fulfilled that promise. Joseph was reunited with his family, but it took twenty-two years. After becoming a Christ-follower, Paul waited three years to begin telling his world about Jesus. It is very hard not to get discouraged when I think about how long I might wait to see our marriage problems resolved. Please help me! Encourage me, God.

Your Word says to wait patiently and confidently when looking forward to something I don't yet have. I want to persevere well. I need more confidence in You. Please renew my strength and help me to wait without fear.

Your love for me includes generous portions of patience. I want to experience Your love so deeply that I am filled with patience toward my husband. Let Your love complete me.

I want to offer my husband a more accurate picture of You. Use me as a reliable messenger of Your great love for him. Your Word says that "patience can persuade a prince." Oh Lord, let Your patience at work within me influence his relationship with You and with me.

I believe You will not waste this trial, God. Allow it to produce patience and endurance in both of us. You are our source of hope. I choose today to keep on praying. Help me to choose this again and again, Lord.

Amen

Declaration

God is my endless source of patience and hope.
He empowers me to persevere with a glad heart.

Scriptures

But if we look forward to something we don't yet have, we must wait patiently and confidently. Romans 8:25

But those who trust in the LORD will find new strength. They will soar high on wings like eagles. They will run and not grow weary. They will walk and not faint. Isaiah 40:31

Be still in the presence of the LORD, and wait patiently for him to act. Don't worry about evil people who prosper or fret about their wicked schemes. Psalm 37:7

Love is patient and kind. 1 Corinthians 13:4a

But the Holy Spirit produces this kind of fruit in our lives: love, joy, peace, patience, kindness, goodness, faithfulness, gentleness, and self-control. There is no law against these things! Galatians 5:22-23

And may you have the power to understand, as all God's people should, how wide, how long, how high, and how deep his love is. May you experience the love of Christ, though it is too great to understand fully. Then you will be made complete with all the fullness of life and power that comes from God. Ephesians 3:18-19

An unreliable messenger stumbles into trouble, but a reliable messenger brings healing. Proverbs 13:17

Patience can persuade a prince, and soft speech can break bones. Proverbs 25:15

For you know that when your faith is tested, your endurance has a chance to grow. So let it grow, for when your endurance is fully developed, you will be perfect and complete, needing nothing. James 1:3-4

We can rejoice, too, when we run into problems and trials, for we know that they help us develop endurance. And endurance develops strength of character, and character strengthens our confident hope of salvation. Romans 5:3-4

Rejoice in our confident hope. Be patient in trouble, and keep on praying. Romans 12:12

Make it Personal

Psalm 37:7 exhorts you to "wait patiently without worry or fear." Study Isaiah 40:29-31 and Isaiah 41:10. Make a list of the promises related to waiting on God to act. Then write a prayer of thanksgiving as if it is already done.

_____

_____

_____

_____

_____

_____

Don't be dejected and
sad, for the joy of the
LORD is your strength!

Nehemiah 8:10b

CHAPTER 15

JOY

God, it has been very difficult for me to be joyful lately. The hard days of this marriage have worn me down, and I don't know how to get my joy back.

Your Word says that my joy will overflow when I accept Your love for me and return it with my obedience to You. Lead me by Your Spirit to focus on pleasing You instead of obsessing about what is wrong in our marriage and who is at fault.

Open my eyes to see You as joyful, God. Help me to trust that joy in the midst of this trial is possible. Teach me to look to You for joy so that I am not lured away from You and this marriage with the many temptations I encounter.

Let the joy of knowing You make me strong. Let Your gift of joy in me bring great delight to my husband.

May we both experience the joy of belonging to You and having access to all we need through our relationship with Jesus.

Amen

Declaration of Faith

The joy of belonging to God sustains me in every situation.

Scriptures References

I have loved you even as the Father has loved me. Remain in my love. When you obey my commandments, you remain in my love, just as I obey my Father's commandments and remain in his love. I have told you these things so that you will be filled with my joy. Yes, your joy will overflow! John 15:9-11

Since we are living by the Spirit, let us follow the Spirit's leading in every part of our lives. Galatians 5:25

For the Kingdom of God is not a matter of what we eat or drink, but of living a life of goodness and peace and joy in the Holy Spirit. Romans 14:17

So letting your sinful nature control your mind leads to death. But letting the Spirit control your mind leads to life and peace. Romans 8:6

Dear brothers and sisters, when troubles come your way, consider it an opportunity for great joy. For you know that when your faith is tested, your endurance has a chance to grow. So let it grow, for when your endurance is fully developed, you will be perfect and complete, needing nothing. James 1:2-4

They are being tested by many troubles, and they are very poor. But they are also filled with abundant joy, which has overflowed in rich generosity. 2 Corinthians 8:2

Don't be dejected and sad, for the joy of the LORD is your strength! Nehemiah 8:10b

You haven't done this before. Ask, using my name, and you will receive, and you will have abundant joy. John 16:24

Make it Personal

Write a prayer asking God to make 2 Corinthians 8:2 a reality in your life.

_____

_____

_____

_____

_____

_____

He led me to a
place of safety; he
rescued me because
he delights in me.

Psalm 18:19

CHAPTER 16

DELIGHT

God, it's been a long time since I was delighted to be married. I really struggle to be content with my husband. Critical and fearful thoughts flood my mind. I feel so weighted down by our struggles. I don't know how to be satisfied in this relationship. Please help me!

Your Word says You delight in those who live Godly lives. I want to live Your way, God. I know that I am not perfect at it. Please help me choose righteousness.

I am thankful that Jesus' righteousness covers me. I believe that You are delighted with Jesus and miraculously, that includes me too. Please help me to perceive Your delight in me. I trust that You can help me hear You singing over me.

I will find delight in You and Your Word so I can be effective in my ministry to my husband, even on the most difficult days. Help me to focus on You, God.

By the power of Your Holy Spirit, help my husband delight in me.

Amen

Declaration of Faith

God is delighted in me, and He enables me to be a delightful wife.

Scripture References

The LORD directs the steps of the godly. He delights in every detail of their lives. Psalm 37:23

I say of the holy people who are in the land, "They are the noble ones in whom is all my delight." Psalm 16:3 NIV

I am overwhelmed with joy in the LORD my God! For he has dressed me with the clothing of salvation and draped me in a robe of righteousness. I am like a bridegroom in his wedding suit or a bride with her jewels. Isaiah 61:10

For our benefit, too, assuring us that God will also count us as righteous if we believe in him, the one who raised Jesus our Lord from the dead. Romans 4:24

For the LORD your God is living among you. He is a mighty savior. He will take delight in you with gladness. With his love, he will calm all your fears. He will rejoice over you with joyful songs. Zephaniah 3:17

Make me walk along the path of your commands, for that is where my happiness is found. Psalm 119:35

But they delight in the law of the LORD, meditating on it day and night. They are like trees planted along the riverbank, bearing fruit each season. Their leaves never wither, and they prosper in all they do. Psalm 1:2-3

The man who finds a wife finds a treasure, and he receives favor from the LORD. Proverbs 18:22

Make it Personal

Study Isaiah 61:10 and Psalm 37:23. Do you see the correlation between your righteousness and God's delight? Take a moment to thank Jesus for His gift of righteousness. Next, talk to God about any doubts you have about His delight in you.

_____

_____

_____

_____

_____

The generous will
prosper; those
who refresh others
will themselves
be refreshed.

▼

Proverbs 11:25

CHAPTER 17

SERVICE

God, there was a time when I really enjoyed serving my spouse. My thoughtfulness was recognized and appreciated. Now, I feel less appreciated than a paid servant.

My heart is bitter and I grumble under my breath when doing even the smallest things. I brace myself knowing I might be criticized for the way I did something. Please help me, God. Help us!

Your Word says I should do everything as if I am serving You, God. I want to do this, but I don't know where to start. I reach for Your hand to guide me.

Please help me forgive my spouse for every snide remark, every dissatisfied comment, and his lack of attention to my efforts. I need

Your forgiveness for my reactions. I need forgiveness for the ways I take my spouse's hard work for granted.

Open my eyes to the way Jesus serves me. I know He is my Prince of Peace, my Wonderful Counselor, my Savior, my Friend, the One who covered my sins with His blood, and so much more. I do not deserve any of this kindness from Him. He is truly the perfect example of choosing to serve and denying oneself for others.

I need Your Holy Spirit to make me an effective helpmate to my spouse. Counsel me to serve in ways that will have a profound impact and meet some of his deepest, even hidden needs. Make me wise and disciplined to pray specifically and persistently. I trust that You have equipped me with good gifts, and You can make them a great blessing to my husband.

Your Word says it is better to give than to receive. I choose a life of giving to my spouse without keeping score.

Amen

Declaration of Faith

I serve my spouse faithfully because in God's kingdom it is better to give than receive.

Scripture References

Work with enthusiasm, as though you were working for the Lord rather than for people. Ephesians 6:7

Whatever you do, work heartily, as for the Lord and not for men, knowing that from the Lord you will receive the inheritance as your reward. You are serving the Lord Christ. Colossians 3:23

But if you do not forgive others their trespasses, neither will your Father forgive your trespasses. Matthew 6:15

Open my eyes to see the wonderful truths in your instructions. Psalm 119:18

For a child is born to us, a son is given to us. The government will rest on his shoulders. And he will be called: Wonderful Counselor, Mighty God, Everlasting Father, Prince of Peace. Isaiah 9:6

He is so rich in kindness and grace that he purchased our freedom with the blood of his Son and forgave our sins. Ephesians 1:7

God has given each of you a gift from his great variety of spiritual gifts. Use them well to serve one another. 1 Peter 4:10

For even the Son of Man came not to be served but to serve others and to give his life as a ransom for many. Matthew 20:28

And the Spirit of the LORD will rest on him--the Spirit of wisdom and understanding, the Spirit of counsel and might, the Spirit of knowledge and the fear of the LORD. Isaiah 11:2

He sat down, called the twelve disciples over to him, and said, "Whoever wants to be first must take last place and be the servant of everyone else." Mark 9:35

Make it Personal

Take time to reflect on how Jesus serves you as Wonderful Counselor, Prince of Peace, Intercessor, and Friend. Record your thoughts in a prayer of thanksgiving.

_____

_____

_____

_____

_____

_____

So again I say, each man must love his wife as he loves himself, and the wife must respect her husband.

Ephesians 5:33

CHAPTER 18

HONOR

Oh God, having marriage problems is embarrassing to me. I often feel shame and regret at what we have become. We have dishonored our vows. We have diminished each other with our words and our behavior. Please forgive both of us. I choose to forgive my husband for every unkind word and act against me.

Teach me, Lord, how to honor him when his behavior is dishonorable. You demonstrated this honor when you approached the woman at the well. You did not hide from her. You showed no disgust of her choices. You spoke to her with gentleness and kindness. You presented the truth about her without shaming her. You simply offered her a different life, the rich life You offer to all of us. Purify my heart, Lord. I want to be able to discuss our areas of conflict without disrespecting him.

My desire is to be a very significant part of the rich and satisfying life You have planned for my husband. Help me not to cooperate with the enemy who would love for my words to destroy his self-image and reputation. Help me follow Your lead, Jesus, and serve Your purposes in this marriage. I choose for myself the honor that comes from serving You.

It is unnatural to love someone who has wronged you. Thank You, Jesus, for showing us a supernatural way to remain loyal to each other. You suffered in order to welcome us into the family of God and fill our lives with the blessings of heaven. Help us honor Your way by offering mercy and taking delight in honoring each other.

God, please fill us with the passion we need to live Your way for the glory of Your great name. I trust that when we do, You will allow honor to abound in our relationship. You are an incredible Father who is able to restore to us double portions of honor for the shame we have endured. I ask You do to that for us now, Lord.

Amen

Declaration of Faith

I make choices that honor God and my spouse.

Scripture References:

Woman at the well – See John 4:1-42

Instead, we will speak the truth in love, growing in every way more and more like Christ, who is the head of his body, the church. Ephesians 4:15

The thief's purpose is to steal and kill and destroy. My purpose is to give them a rich and satisfying life. John 10:10

Anyone who wants to be my disciple must follow me, because my servants must be where I am. And the Father will honor anyone who serves me. John 12:26

Love each other with genuine affection, and take delight in honoring each other. Romans 12:10

Whoever pursues righteousness and unfailing love will find life, righteousness, and honor. Proverbs 21:21

Instead of shame and dishonor, you will enjoy a double share of honor. You will possess a double portion of prosperity in your land, and everlasting joy will be yours. Isaiah 61:7

Make it Personal

God instructs wives to show respect (another word for honor) to their husbands (Ephesians 5:33). Invite God to reveal to you specific ways to respect to your husband. Make a list of the ideas that come to you. Pray over each one asking God to prepare your husband to recognize the way you honored him and receive the blessing.

_____

_____

_____

_____

_____

Make every effort
to keep yourselves
united in the Spirit,
binding yourselves
together with peace.

———▼———

Ephesians 4:3

CHAPTER 19

UNITY

God, there is a force more powerful than me trying to divide us. I want so badly to be one with my husband, but my thoughts carry me away from him instead. I've allowed anger, bitterness, and resentment to erect walls between us. I've been too offended to move toward him. I've been too stressed and self-focused to notice him. My own pride has eaten away at the fabric of our marriage like an acid.

Our attempts to move toward each other often erupt into arguments. Nothing gets resolved. The wounds just get deeper. You are our only hope, God.

Please forgive me for exalting my way of doing life as the perfect way. Please change my narrow-minded thinking so my choices are good for us not just me. Please forgive my husband for doing the same things.

Help us both honor Your way by being kind, gentle, patient, humble and merciful with each other.

It is very difficult to feel united with someone who is rejecting me. Obviously it is not impossible, because You have chosen to remain united with me in my worst moments. Thank You! I am in awe of the gift of Your faithfulness to me. God. I want to honor You by pursuing peace with my husband at all times.

My eyes are on You, God. I am listening for Your Holy Spirit's promptings to move toward him with respect. I am ready to deny my feelings a right to rule over me. You are Lord and Master. I choose Your way because I want to become a steady source of peace in our relationship.

Teach me to think of him as a part of me that needs support the same way an arm needs the support of a shoulder. Help him to see my supportive role as a critical component to his good life.

Create in us, Lord, a determined spirit to resist every temptation to be divided including the authoritative whispers of our parents, the media and our closest influencers. Make us wise and willing to put firm boundaries in place.

On the cross, You demonstrated Your power to demolish the division between Jews and Gentiles. I am filled with hope that You are able to cause the walls between us to fall like the great wall of Jericho.

Amen

Declaration of Faith

With God's power, I resist every divisive thought about my husband and our marriage.

Scripture References

For we are not fighting against flesh-and-blood enemies, but against evil rulers and authorities of the unseen world, against mighty powers in this dark world, and against evil spirits in the heavenly places.
Ephesians 6:12

Get rid of all bitterness, rage, anger, harsh words, and slander, as well as all types of evil behavior. Ephesians 4:31

Sensible people control their temper; they earn respect by overlooking wrongs. Proverbs 19:11

Pride goes before destruction, and haughtiness before a fall.
Proverbs 16:18

Yes, I am the vine; you are the branches. Those who remain in me, and I in them, will produce much fruit. For apart from me you can do nothing.
John 15:5

Live in harmony with each other. Don't be too proud to enjoy the company of ordinary people. And don't think you know it all!
Romans 12:16

Since God chose you to be the holy people he loves, you must clothe yourselves with tenderhearted mercy, kindness, humility, gentleness, and patience. Make allowance for each other's faults, and forgive anyone who offends you. Remember, the Lord forgave you, so you must forgive others. Above all, clothe yourselves with love, which binds us all together in perfect harmony. Colossians 3:12-14

Work at living in peace with everyone, and work at living a holy life, for those who are not holy will not see the Lord. Hebrews 12:14

Do all that you can to live in peace with everyone. Romans 12:18

So again I say, each man must love his wife as he loves himself, and the wife must respect her husband. Ephesians 5:33

And this righteousness will bring peace. Yes, it will bring quietness and confidence forever. Isaiah 32:17

Oh, the joys of those who do not follow the advice of the wicked, or stand around with sinners, or join in with mockers. But they delight in the law of the LORD, meditating on it day and night. They are like trees planted along the riverbank, bearing fruit each season. Their leaves never wither, and they prosper in all they do. Psalm 1:1-3

Then the LORD God said, "It is not good for the man to be alone. I will make a helper who is just right for him." Genesis 2:18

'This explains why a man leaves his father and mother and is joined to his wife, and the two are united into one.' Since they are no longer two but one, let no one split apart what God has joined together." Mark 10:7-9

For Christ himself has brought peace to us. He united Jews and Gentiles into one people when, in his own body on the cross, he broke down the wall of hostility that separated us. Ephesians 2:14

It was by faith that the people of Israel marched around Jericho for seven days, and the walls came crashing down. Hebrews 11:30

Make it Personal

Are there people in your lives who encourage division between you and your husband? Take a moment to write a prayer of forgiveness for them. Ask God to help you recognize any other outside source of division. Next invite God to guide you in establishing protective boundaries for your marriage.

_____

_____

_____

_____

_____

_____

Wait patiently for
the LORD. Be brave
and courageous.
Yes, wait patiently
for the LORD.

Psalm 27:14

CHAPTER 20

COURAGE

God, I'm so tired of being fearful about our future. I've become hesitant and doubtful in decision-making. I want to be a woman of great courage. I want to be bold in prayer, in faith, and in my decisions. Help me not to be double minded by asking You to restore our marriage and then worrying that You can't or won't.

Please forgive me for entertaining timidity as if it were a friend. I am sorry that I have cooperated with the enemy of my soul in this way. I've dishonored Your name by acting as if You would desert me and fail to help me.

I choose today to put my hope in You, Lord! I choose the life of strength and courage Joshua and Caleb modeled on their covert mission in the Promised Land.

With the help of Your Spirit, I will not fear bad news. I choose the peace that comes from keeping my mind fixed on Your character and Your faithfulness to me.

God, I ask You to help my husband rely on You for strength and courage as well. Help him boast about his fears to You so he can receive the strength You are always offering him.

Amen

Declaration of Faith

The strength and courage of Jesus are alive within me.

Scripture References

The wicked run away when no one is chasing them, but the godly are as bold as lions. Proverbs 28:1

But when you ask him, be sure that your faith is in God alone. Do not waver, for a person with divided loyalty is as unsettled as a wave of the sea that is blown and tossed by the wind. James 1:6

For God has not given us a spirit of fear and timidity, but of power, love, and self-discipline. 2 Timothy 1:7

So be strong and courageous! Do not be afraid and do not panic before them. For the LORD your God will personally go ahead of you. He will neither fail you nor abandon you. Deuteronomy 31:6

So be strong and courageous, all you who put your hope in the LORD!
Psalm 31:24

Joshua and Caleb - Numbers 13, 14

They do not fear bad news; they confidently trust the LORD to care for them. Psalm 112:7

You will keep in perfect peace all who trust in you, all whose thoughts are fixed on you! Isaiah 26:3

Each time he said, "My grace is all you need. My power works best in weakness." So now I am glad to boast about my weaknesses, so that the power of Christ can work through me. 2 Corinthians 12:9

Make it Personal

Are you prone to fear bad news? Psalm 112:7 relates this fear to a lack of confident trust in God. Write a prayer to God asking Him to increase your confidence in His promise to take care of you despite your imperfect circumstances.

_____

_____

_____

_____

_____

_____

If I could speak all
the languages of earth
and of angels, but didn't
love others, I would only
be a noisy gong or a
clanging cymbal.

1 Corinthians 13:1

CHAPTER 21

LOVE YOUR ENEMIES

Oh God, there are moments in this marriage when my husband and I war against each other like enemies. Anger and even hatred swell in my heart towards him. My defenses go up, and I move further away from him in my heart.

Your Word instructs me to love my enemy. How is this possible? How do I act lovingly when he doesn't deserve it? How do I give love when my feelings are the exact opposite? How do I give him my body when he keeps pushing me further and further away with his words and actions?

Show me how to be good to him, Lord. Inspire me to pray for him. Help me turn the other cheek and treat him the way I want to be treated. I resist the prideful thought that I should only serve him when he is serving me. You are kind to the unthankful and the wicked. Let Your compassionate ways be my ways, Lord.

God, help me keep my mind focused on You and my heart set on pleasing You instead of myself. I trust that pleasing You will bring peace into our relationship. Thank You for allowing Jesus to die for me while I was Your enemy. I am grateful that He made a way for me to be at peace with You!

Lead me by Your Spirit to be honest *and* loving. Inspire me to set boundaries when necessary. Grant me favor with my husband. You are able to help him respect the boundaries. I believe you are able to change his heart toward me and my heart toward him. Nothing is impossible with You!

Amen

Declaration of Faith

I choose to love to my husband even when he feels like my enemy.

Scripture References

But to you who are willing to listen, I say, love your enemies! Do good to those who hate you. Bless those who curse you. Pray for those who hurt you. If someone slaps you on one cheek, offer the other cheek also. If someone demands your coat, offer your shirt also. Give to anyone who asks; and when things are taken away from you, don't try to get them back. Do to others as you would like them to do to you. If you love only those who love you, why should you get credit for that? Even sinners love those who love them! And if you do good only to those who do good to you, why should you get credit? Even sinners do that much! And if you lend money only to those who can repay you, why should you get credit? Even sinners will lend to other sinners for a full return. Love your enemies! Do good to them. Lend to them without expecting to be repaid. Then your reward from heaven will be very great, and you will truly be acting as children of the Most High, for he is kind to those who are unthankful and wicked. You must be compassionate, just as your Father is compassionate. Luke 6:27-36

We destroy arguments and every lofty opinion raised against the knowledge of God, and take every thought captive to obey Christ, 2 Corinthians 10:5 ESV

You will keep in perfect peace all who trust in you, all whose thoughts are fixed on you! Isaiah 26:3

Obviously, I'm not trying to win the approval of people, but of God. If pleasing people were my goal, I would not be Christ's servant. Galatians 1:10

When people's lives please the LORD, even their enemies are at peace with them. Proverbs 16:7

Instead, we will speak the truth in love, growing in every way more and more like Christ, who is the head of his body, the church. Ephesians 4:15

For since our friendship with God was restored by the death of his Son while we were still his enemies, we will certainly be saved through the life of his Son. Romans 5:10

And I will give you a new heart, and I will put a new spirit in you. I will take out your stony, stubborn heart and give you a tender, responsive heart. Ezekiel 36:26

For nothing is impossible with God. Luke 1:37

Make it Personal

Do you know someone who has chosen to love an enemy? Thank God for giving you a good example of living His way. Do you know Christians who have chosen not to live by Luke 6:27-36? Ask God to forgive them and to help you choose differently.

_____

_____

_____

_____

_____

_____

SECTION 4: FIGHT FOR FREEDOM FROM STRONGHOLDS

There are giants in your promised land. They loom over you threatening complete annihilation of your marriage. Thankfully we have the courageous examples of Joshua, Caleb, and David to teach us how to handle them.

Joshua and Caleb's team of spies gave up on living in their promised land because the giants made them look like grasshoppers. They were afraid! The only reason Joshua and Caleb were willing to venture into the giant infested land of blessing was their faith in God's power over those giants.

Consider David's bold approach to Goliath. He was a brave young boy surrounded by fearful warriors. His faith in God was so strong. The smallness of his weapons did not worry him. Previous fights against lions and bear proved to him that God was with him and would fight for him. With supernatural boldness, David pursued victory over the voice mocking God's name and His people.

Your giants are no match for God. Let your faith in God's power to defeat every force of evil rise up. You may feel small and hopeless, but like Gideon, God calls you a mighty warrior (Judges 6:12).

We use God's mighty weapons, not worldly weapons, to knock down the strongholds of human reasoning and to destroy false arguments. We destroy every proud obstacle that keeps people from knowing God. We capture their rebellious thoughts and teach them to obey Christ.
2 Corinthians 10:4-5

The eternal God is your refuge, and his everlasting arms are under you. He drives out the enemy before you; he cries out, 'Destroy them!'
Deuteronomy 33:27

The name of the LORD is a strong fortress; the godly run to him and are safe.
Proverbs 18:10

The wicked run away when no one is chasing them, but the godly are as bold as lions.
Proverbs 28:1

Unfailing love and truth
have met together.
Righteousness and
peace have kissed!

Psalm 85:10

CHAPTER 22

HIDDEN SIN

God, our marriage feels like it's hanging on a thread. I'm panicking, and he appears to have no interest in change. When I talk about our issues, he responds with anger or acts like I am crazy for thinking something is wrong.

I have this sick feeling he is hiding something from me. Maybe he thinks he is hiding it from You, but You see all things. Even the deepest hidden sin is known by You.

There is a part of me that wants to hide too. I imagine the worst is happening. Will I be devastated? Will the truth set us free or be the end of us? Help me, God. I don't want my own fears to inflame this situation even more. Help me to know You in a way that diminishes my fear.

You are the God who reveals hidden things. I invite You to reveal to my husband that You are with him, You see him, and Your love for him has not waned. Help him to feel safe with You so he is able to confess his sins, turn from them, and receive mercy from You. Make me ready to be merciful, kind, humble, gentle and patient with him as well. I want to be a safe place for him.

In the name of Jesus, I speak to his heart and call him awake to You, God. I call him awake to his sin. Let his eyes be wide open. Help him to clothe himself with the strength You offer him, Lord. Where he has been weak to fight the temptations bombarding his mind, I know You are able to fight for him and with him. You are the victorious God, and You cause him to be more than a conqueror.

Cleanse both of us from any hidden faults, God. Create in us clean hearts. Let our love for You and Your Word multiply so that we are driven to live holy, blameless lives together.

Amen

Declaration of Faith

God is able to reveal what is hidden, heal what is broken, and transform a wicked heart.

Scripture References

I am watching them closely, and I see every sin. They cannot hope to hide from me. Jeremiah 16:7

I could ask the darkness to hide me and the light around me to become night--but even in darkness I cannot hide from you. To you the night

shines as bright as day. Darkness and light are the same to you.
Psalm 139:11-12

And you will know the truth, and the truth will set you free. John 8:32

Don't be afraid, for I am with you. Don't be discouraged, for I am your God. I will strengthen you and help you. I will hold you up with my victorious right hand. Isaiah 41:10

He reveals deep and mysterious things and knows what lies hidden in darkness, though he is surrounded by light. Daniel 2:22

People who conceal their sins will not prosper, but if they confess and turn from them, they will receive mercy. Proverbs 28:13

Since God chose you to be the holy people he loves, you must clothe yourselves with tenderhearted mercy, kindness, humility, gentleness, and patience. Colossians 3:12

Wake up, wake up, O Zion! Clothe yourself with strength. Put on your beautiful clothes, O holy city of Jerusalem, for unclean and godless people will enter your gates no longer. Isaiah 52:1

The LORD himself will fight for you. Just stay calm. Exodus 14:14

No, despite all these things, overwhelming victory is ours through Christ, who loved us. Romans 8:37

How can I know all the sins lurking in my heart? Cleanse me from these hidden faults. Psalm 19:12

Create in me a clean heart, O God. Renew a loyal spirit within me.
Psalm 51:10

Make them holy by your truth; teach them your word, which is truth.
John 17:17

Make it Personal

Write a prayer for your husband based on Isaiah 52:1. Think of all the strengths God has to fill in the gaps of his weaknesses. Invite God to help you believe this is all possible.

_____

_____

_____

_____

_____

_____

He heals the
brokenhearted
and bandages
their wounds.

———————▼———————

Psalm 147:3

CHAPTER 23

REJECTION

God, I feel so rejected. The pain is almost unbearable at times. How could this happen? We chose each other for better or worse. How do I choose to love someone who rejects me?

My heart is broken and my spirits are so low. I need Your healing touch. My husband does too.

Your Word says that I do not wrestle against flesh and blood, but against evil forces. I understand there is a spiritual war against my marriage, and the evil one is at work to divide us. I embrace the reality that my husband is not my enemy. Please help him see this spiritual reality and make the same choice.

Jesus, you were despised and rejected. I am grateful You understand how I feel. At times, I have rejected Your love and Your sacrifice. Please forgive me. I have also caused my husband to feel rejected. Please forgive me, Lord. Help him to forgive me too.

You are the Almighty God. I trust in Your resurrection power to restore loving kindness and passion in our sacred union. Nothing is impossible for You. Our hurt feelings, self-protective stances, and harsh words are no match for Your restoration power.

I will wait on You to reverse the direction of our marriage. I am awake to Your voice, and I am clothed with the strength that You provide. I place my trust in Jesus who causes me to be more than a conqueror in this painful season.

Amen

Declaration of Faith

I am chosen and loved by God. I give no place to feelings of rejection.

Scripture References

The LORD is close to the brokenhearted; he rescues those whose spirits are crushed. Psalm 34:18

For we are not fighting against flesh-and-blood enemies, but against evil rulers and authorities of the unseen world, against mighty powers in this dark world, and against evil spirits in the heavenly places. Ephesians 6:12

He was despised and rejected--a man of sorrows, acquainted with deepest grief. We turned our backs on him and looked the other way. He was despised, and we did not care. Isaiah 53:3

But if we confess our sins to him, he is faithful and just to forgive us our sins and to cleanse us from all wickedness. 1 John 1:9

I also pray that you will understand the incredible greatness of God's power for us who believe him. This is the same mighty power that raised Christ from the dead and seated him in the place of honor at God's right hand in the heavenly realms. Ephesians 1:19-20

For nothing is impossible with God. Luke 1:37

O Sovereign LORD! You made the heavens and earth by your strong hand and powerful arm. Nothing is too hard for you! Jeremiah 32:17

But those who trust in the LORD will find new strength. They will soar high on wings like eagles. They will run and not grow weary. They will walk and not faint. Isaiah 40:31

Wake up, wake up, O Zion! Clothe yourself with strength. Put on your beautiful clothes, O holy city of Jerusalem, for unclean and godless people will enter your gates no longer. Isaiah 52:1

No, despite all these things, overwhelming victory is ours through Christ, who loved us. Romans 8:37

Make it Personal

Write a prayer thanking God for His promise never to forsake or reject you. Use Deuteronomy 31:6 and Psalm 94:14 as the foundation of your prayer. Go a step further and write a declaration of God's faithfulness to you in the midst of the present rejection you are experiencing. Here is an example: "My husband may reject me, but God created me and values me as the temple of His Holy Spirit. He delights in every detail of my life."

_____

_____

_____

_____

_____

_____

When the poor and needy
search for water and there
is none, and their tongues are
parched from thirst, then I,
the LORD, will answer them.
I, the God of Israel, will
never abandon them.

———————▼———————

Isaiah 41:17

CHAPTER 24

DESPERATE FOR LOVE

God, I never expected to feel this empty and desperate for something different. My soul is so connected to my spouse, but our minds and bodies are very disconnected. This war between us leaves me thirsty for love.

With my own voice, I vowed to be faithful in every way. How can I resist this unrelenting desire to connect with love when none is evident within our marriage? My heart cries out for affection. My soul tells me I deserve better than this. My mind suggests that I should find someone who does love me. This temptation to pursue another is fierce.

Here is my heart, Lord. I'm in great need of Your perfect love. Help me believe that You will supply all of my needs, even this one. I reach for You to satisfy my soul.

I choose to honor the righteousness of Jesus by keeping our marriage bed pure. By the power of Your Holy Spirit, I will deny myself what the world offers, so I can receive all that You have to give us. Please help my husband do the same.

You are the river of living waters. My soul is refreshed by You and the good gifts You give. I will wait in the shelter of Your wing for love to overflow between us.

Declaration of Faith

God meets my needs with His love. He empowers me
to wait for love to return to our marriage.

Scripture References

And this same God who takes care of me will supply all your needs from his glorious riches, which have been given to us in Christ Jesus. Philippians 4:19

I lift my hands to you in prayer. I thirst for you as parched land thirsts for rain. Interlude. Come quickly, LORD, and answer me, for my depression deepens. Don't turn away from me, or I will die. Psalm 143:6-7

Give honor to marriage, and remain faithful to one another in marriage. God will surely judge people who are immoral and those who commit adultery. Hebrews 13:4

And we are instructed to turn from godless living and sinful pleasures. We should live in this evil world with wisdom, righteousness, and devotion to God, Titus 2:12

For you bless the righteous, O LORD; you cover him with favor as with a shield. Psalm 5:12 ESV

Whatever is good and perfect comes down to us from God our Father, who created all the lights in the heavens. He never changes or casts a shifting shadow. James 1:17

Anyone who believes in me may come and drink! For the Scriptures declare, 'Rivers of living water will flow from his heart.' John 7:38

He will cover you with his feathers. He will shelter you with his wings. His faithful promises are your armor and protection. Psalm 91:4

I pray that your love will overflow more and more, and that you will keep on growing in knowledge and understanding. Philippians 1:9

Make it Personal

Search the Bible for evidence that God can satisfy your need for love. Start with Psalm 103:5 and Ephesians 3:18-19. Write a prayer to God expressing your need for love and inviting Him to meet it.

_____

_____

_____

_____

_____

But now is the
time to get rid of
anger, rage, malicious
behavior, slander,
and dirty language.

Colossians 3:8

CHAPTER 25

ANGER

God, what do I do with all of this anger I feel toward my husband?

Your Word says I can be angry as long as I do not let the anger lead me into sin. We have both failed at this far too often. Please forgive us. Please help us!

With a weary heart, I bring my anger, rage, bitterness and resentment to You. You are the safest place I have to be honest about how I feel, God. Thank You for knowing my every thought and still loving me.

Heal my heart, Lord. Save me. Save us from the destruction my anger brings to this marriage. Please do the same for my husband and his anger, Lord.

Pour out on us Your wisdom and insight. Wake us up to the right way to handle fear, disappointments, and offenses. Clothe us with Your strength to respond with a soft answer and Your wisdom. Retrain our minds so that we are quick to listen to each other and slow to make assumptions and give solutions. Slay our pride, Lord, so our every communication is delivered with humility and openness to correction.

Thank You, God, for the great hope I have in Your power to transform us in this way.

Amen

Declaration of Faith

God makes me wise to respond to conflict with gentleness and humility.

Scripture References

Be angry and do not sin. Don't let the sun go down on your anger, Ephesians 4:26 HCSB

Human anger does not produce the righteousness God desires. James 1:20

But now is the time to get rid of anger, rage, malicious behavior, slander, and dirty language. Colossians 3:8

You know when I sit down or stand up. You know my thoughts even when I'm far away. Psalm 139:2

O LORD, if you heal me, I will be truly healed; if you save me, I will be truly saved. My praises are for you alone! Jeremiah 17:14

And the tongue is a flame of fire. It is a whole world of wickedness, corrupting your entire body. It can set your whole life on fire, for it is set on fire by hell itself. James 3:6

... asking God, the glorious Father of our Lord Jesus Christ, to give you spiritual wisdom and insight so that you might grow in your knowledge of God. Ephesians 1:17

Wake up, wake up, O Zion! Clothe yourself with strength. Put on your beautiful clothes, O holy city of Jerusalem, for unclean and godless people will enter your gates no longer. Isaiah 52:1

A gentle answer deflects anger, but harsh words make tempers flare. Proverbs 15:1

Understand this, my dear brothers and sisters: You must all be quick to listen, slow to speak, and slow to get angry. James 1:19

Pride leads to conflict; those who take advice are wise. Proverbs 13:10

Make it Personal

Review the following passages. Write your own prayer based on the ones that fit your present need.

Psalm 37:8
Proverbs 19:11,19
Proverbs 29:11

And don't let us
yield to temptation,
but rescue us from
the evil one.

Matthew 6:13

CHAPTER 26

ADDICTION

What do I do, God? This addiction has robbed us of so much. Before it, we communicated freely. We were connected emotionally. We were on the same page about most things. Lying, hiding, and isolation walked in the door with this addiction and everything changed.

I have never felt so powerless, God. I feel rejected. I just want this to be over! Please help us before it completely devours him and our marriage.

You are the Almighty God. You gave the Shunammite woman a son and when he died, You used Elisha to bring His dead body back to life. You have given me a husband, and now I need You to send an Elisha to bring him back to this marriage.

Holy Spirit, please awaken my husband to see his sin and captivity. Clothe him with strength and humility. Help him call on the name of Jesus and be saved. Help him resist the enemy and draw close to You, God.

Rescue him from this evil scheme, Lord. You separated the Israelites from their enemies by parting the Red Sea and allowing it to swallow their enemies. Please separate my husband from his temptations in the same way. You are the God who hears my prayers. You are the God who causes enemies to be disgraced and retreat in shame.

Only You know the pain, the memories, and the shame in his heart that brought him to this place of relying on something other than You. Only You can heal him and set him free. You are the one who causes beauty to rise up out of the ashes.

Awaken self-control within him, Holy Spirit. Enable him to resist temptation with the same steadfastness that Daniel and his friends exercised to resist the king's rich foods.

My hope for him and our marriage is anchored in Your promise that overwhelming victory is possible because of Christ Jesus.

Declaration of Faith

Addiction is no match for my God.

Scripture References

Resurrection of the Shunammite's son -- 2 Kings 4:31-37

Wake up, wake up, O Zion! Clothe yourself with strength. Put on your beautiful clothes, O holy city of Jerusalem, for unclean and godless people will enter your gates no longer. Isaiah 52:1

Since God chose you to be the holy people he loves, you must clothe yourselves with tenderhearted mercy, kindness, humility, gentleness, and patience. Colossians 3:12

For "Everyone who calls on the name of the LORD will be saved." Romans 10:13

Therefore submit to God. Resist the devil and he will flee from you. Draw near to God and He will draw near to you. Cleanse your hands, you sinners; and purify your hearts, you double-minded. James 4:7-8

Then call on me when you are in trouble, and I will rescue you, and you will give me glory. Psalm 50:15

And don't let us yield to temptation, but rescue us from the evil one. Matthew 6:13

The temptations in your life are no different from what others experience. And God is faithful. He will not allow the temptation to be more than you can stand. When you are tempted, he will show you a way out so that you can endure. 1 Corinthians 10:13

But Moses told the people, "Don't be afraid. Just stand still and watch the LORD rescue you today. The Egyptians you see today will never be seen again. The LORD himself will fight for you. Just stay calm (Exodus 14:13-14). Read all of Exodus 14 for the full story of the Israelites crossing the Red Sea.

The LORD has heard my plea; the LORD will answer my prayer. May all my enemies be disgraced and terrified. May they suddenly turn back in shame. Psalm 6:9-10

To all who mourn in Israel, he will give a crown of beauty for ashes, a joyous blessing instead of mourning, festive praise instead of despair. In their righteousness, they will be like great oaks that the LORD has planted for his own glory. Isaiah 61:3

But the Holy Spirit produces this kind of fruit in our lives: love, joy, peace, patience, kindness, goodness, faithfulness, gentleness, and self-control. There is no law against these things! Galatians 5:22-23

But Daniel was determined not to defile himself by eating the food and wine given to them by the king. He asked the chief of staff for permission not to eat these unacceptable foods. Daniel 1:8

This hope is a strong and trustworthy anchor for our souls. It leads us through the curtain into God's inner sanctuary. Hebrews 6:19

No, despite all these things, overwhelming victory is ours through Christ, who loved us. Romans 8:37

Make it Personal

Addiction often stems from a choice to self-medicate emotional pain. Invite God to reveal Himself to your spouse as his Healer. Write a prayer asking God to remove the poison left in his heart by traumatic experiences and replace it with the reality of redemption. If you struggle with an addiction, rewrite the above prayer for yourself.

They kept demanding an
answer, so he stood up again
and said, "All right, but let the
one who has never sinned
throw the first stone!"

———————▼———————

John 8:7

CHAPTER 27

FAULT FINDING

Help me God! I have become an expert on everything that is wrong with my husband. My thoughts and words about him are harsh and negative.

I promised to love him for better or worse. I just don't know what to do with the worst. I feel powerless to change him and the way I think and feel about him.

Please forgive me. You've instructed me to focus my attention on my own failings before I gently and humbly talk to him about his weaknesses. I am guilty of ignoring my own wicked heart and pointing the finger at him. Help me turn my focus back to the only person I can change - me!

I have cooperated with Satan's plan to destroy my husband by stoning him with my thoughts and words. I have tolerated attacks on his character by close friends and family. I have forsaken my vow to do good to him all the days of our life together.

Teach me, Lord, to fight for him and not against him. Help me live in complete agreement with Your loving kindness towards him.

Make me merciful instead of judgmental. Forgive me for judging myself better than him. We are both in great need of Your strength to cover our weaknesses.

Make me an accurate reflection of Jesus who gave his entire life to helping people and saving them from judgment.

Amen

Declaration of Faith

I am in great need of mercy, so I freely give it to my husband.

Scripture References

Don't grumble about each other, brothers and sisters, or you will be judged. For look--the Judge is standing at the door! James 5:9

Do not judge, or you too will be judged. For you will be treated as you treat others. The standard you use in judging is the standard by which you will be judged. "And why worry about a speck in your friend's eye when you have a log in your own? How can you think of saying to your friend, 'Let me help you get rid of that speck in your eye,' when you can't see past the log in your own eye? Hypocrite! First get rid of the log in your own eye; then you will see well enough to deal with the speck in your friend's eye. Matthew 7:1-5

Dear brothers and sisters, if another believer is overcome by some sin, you who are godly should gently and humbly help that person back onto the right path. And be careful not to fall into the same temptation yourself. Galatians 6:1

The thief's purpose is to steal and kill and destroy. My purpose is to give them a rich and satisfying life. John 10:10

The tongue can bring death or life; those who love to talk will reap the consequences. Proverbs 18:21

Your unfailing love is better than life itself; how I praise you! Psalm 63:3

Do not judge others, and you will not be judged. Do not condemn others, or it will all come back against you. Forgive others, and you will be forgiven. Luke 6:37

Because of the privilege and authority God has given me, I give each of you this warning: Don't think you are better than you really are. Be honest in your evaluation of yourselves, measuring yourselves by the faith God has given us. Romans 12:3

For what gives you the right to make such a judgment? What do you have that God hasn't given you? And if everything you have is from God, why boast as though it were not a gift? 1 Corinthians 4:7

Don't speak evil against each other, dear brothers and sisters. If you criticize and judge each other, then you are criticizing and judging God's law. But your job is to obey the law, not to judge whether it applies to you. God alone, who gave the law, is the Judge. He alone has the power to save or to destroy. So what right do you have to judge your neighbor? James 4:11-12

Each time he said, "My grace is all you need. My power works best in weakness." So now I am glad to boast about my weaknesses, so that the power of Christ can work through me. 2 Corinthians 12:9

God sent his Son into the world not to judge the world, but to save the world through him. John 3:17

Make it Personal

We can often trace a critical, faultfinding spirit to a desperate desire to please God with our own perfection. Are you trying to earn His approval, or do you believe Jesus did that for you on the cross? Write a prayer inviting God to show you if you are working to please Him without first believing that He is pleased with you.

_____

_____

_____

_____

_____

_____

For the Lord is the Spirit, and wherever the Spirit of the Lord is, there is freedom.

2 Corinthians 3:17

CHAPTER 28

CONTROL AND MANIPULATION

God, I think we are both trying to bring stability and order into our marriage the wrong way. I never wanted marriage to be this way for us. I'm really struggling to like him. I know I'm supposed to respect him, but I'm so angry about how he treats me. This is a twisted sense of oneness. Only You can bring peace and unity into this mess.

I confess to You, God, that I often hide the truth to control the atmosphere in our household and our circumstances. I have cowered in fear of his reaction to my thoughts and feelings. I am guilty of creating a false sense of unity and peace. Please forgive me.

You know all things. I know You have seen and heard me each time I have tried to hurt him before his words could hurt me. Please forgive me for manipulating the conversation by raising my voice and talking down to my husband.

I've chosen to control and manipulate because I felt someone had to do something to right the wrongs in our marriage. Please forgive me for employing the world's ways instead of seeking You for answers and change. I surrender my mind and personality to You. I relinquish control to You, Lord.

God, my husband tries to control me by withholding attention, affection, money, and my right to give input into important conversations. His words can cut me like a knife. His lack of communication hurts me just as much.

I choose to forgive him. I recognize that he is human and my fight is not against him, but the enemy of our souls and our marriage. I bring to You his fears, his lack of spiritual insight, and the patterns he learned from his family of origin. I ask You to strengthen him where he is weak. I ask You to help Him leave all of this behind and walk in the wisdom You provide. Help me do the same.

Your Word says we are to be subject to one another. I trust You are able to change our hearts and minds. Nothing is too hard for You, God. Send Your Word to heal us and deliver us from our destructive ways.

Amen

Declaration of Faith

I release all control in this marriage into the hands of God.

Scripture References

So again I say, each man must love his wife as he loves himself, and the wife must respect her husband. Ephesians 5:33

I am leaving you with a gift--peace of mind and heart. And the peace I give is a gift the world cannot give. So don't be troubled or afraid. John 14:27

Make every effort to keep yourselves united in the Spirit, binding yourselves together with peace. Ephesians 4:3

Don't lie to each other, for you have stripped off your old sinful nature and all its wicked deeds. Colossians 3:9

The wicked run away when no one is chasing them, but the godly are as bold as lions. Proverbs 28:1

But the LORD was with Joseph in the prison and showed him his faithful love. And the LORD made Joseph a favorite with the prison warden. Genesis 39:21

You see me when I travel and when I rest at home. You know everything I do. You know what I am going to say even before I say it, LORD. Psalm 139:3-4

So encourage each other and build each other up, just as you are already doing. 1 Thessalonians 5:11

"My thoughts are nothing like your thoughts," says the LORD. "And my ways are far beyond anything you could imagine. For just as the heavens are higher than the earth, so my ways are higher than your ways and my thoughts higher than your thoughts." Isaiah 55:8-9

For we are not fighting against flesh-and-blood enemies, but against evil rulers and authorities of the unseen world, against mighty powers in this dark world, and against evil spirits in the heavenly places.
Ephesians 6:12

And further, submit to one another out of reverence for Christ.
Ephesians 5:21

I am the LORD, the God of all the peoples of the world. Is anything too hard for me? Jeremiah 32:27

He sent out his word and healed them, snatching them from the door of death. Psalm 107:20

Make it Personal

Jezebel was a controlling, demanding, and manipulative wife. Read about her in 1 Kings chapters 16, 18, 19, and 21. Take note of what she did to get her way. Invite the Holy Spirit to convict you of any similar attitudes and activities. Declare to God your desire to resist all her evil ways.

_____

_____

_____

_____

_____

_____

Whoever gives to the poor will lack nothing, but those who close their eyes to poverty will be cursed.

Proverbs 28:27

CHAPTER 29

FINANCIAL PROBLEMS

God, I am so worried about our finances. We have struggled for so long to make more than we spend. My husband and I never seem to be on the same page about how to spend and when to save. Our debt feels like a millstone around my neck.

You promised to satisfy the needs of those who live godly lives. Open the eyes of our hearts to see our ungodly choices. Show us where our financial choices have been motivated by greed, envy, and a strong desire to fit in with others. Do we love money more than we want to please You? Are we lazy and entitled? Let the conviction of Your Holy Spirit burn in our hearts.

Help us to think Your thoughts about money. Spark our enthusiasm to honor You with tithes and offerings. Increase our faith in Your promise to sustain us financially when we prioritize Your kingdom. Fill us with Your compassion for widows, orphans, and the needy. Unite us in providing for them and especially our own family when they are in need.

Help us choose a life of working diligently as if we are working for You, God. Rid us of any laziness that sets us up for poverty. Empower us with Your wisdom to avoid get-rich-quick schemes. You are the One who enables us to earn wealth. I am drawing near to You now in great need of Your promised help.

Forgive us for making, saving, and spending money outside of Your will. I choose for us the humility and respect for You that leads us to riches, honor, and a long life. I ask You for more freedom for us so we can experience Your promised prosperity.

Amen

Declaration of Faith

I follow God's wisdom in money matters and rely on Him to lead my husband to do the same.

Scripture References

The LORD will not let the godly go hungry, but he refuses to satisfy the craving of the wicked. Proverbs 10:3

Once I was young, and now I am old. Yet I have never seen the godly abandoned or their children begging for bread. Psalm 37:25

Then he said, "Beware! Guard against every kind of greed. Life is not measured by how much you own." Luke 12:15

A peaceful heart leads to a healthy body; jealousy is like cancer in the bones. Proverbs 14:30

Don't love money; be satisfied with what you have. For God has said, "I will never fail you. I will never abandon you." Hebrews 13:5

Lazy people want much but get little, but those who work hard will prosper. Proverbs 13:4

So the LORD sparked the enthusiasm of Zerubbabel son of Shealtiel, governor of Judah, and the enthusiasm of Jeshua son of Jehozadak, the high priest, and the enthusiasm of the whole remnant of God's people. They began to work on the house of their God, the LORD of Heaven's Armies, ... Haggai 1:14

Bring all the tithes into the storehouse so there will be enough food in my Temple. If you do," says the LORD of Heaven's Armies, "I will open the windows of heaven for you. I will pour out a blessing so great you won't have enough room to take it in! Try it! Put me to the test! Malachi 3:10

Pure and genuine religion in the sight of God the Father means caring for orphans and widows in their distress and refusing to let the world corrupt you. James 1:27

But those who won't care for their relatives, especially those in their own household, have denied the true faith. Such people are worse than unbelievers. 1 Timothy 5:8

Work willingly at whatever you do, as though you were working for the Lord rather than for people. Colossians 3:23

Lazy people are soon poor; hard workers get rich. Proverbs 10:4

Wealth from get-rich-quick schemes quickly disappears; wealth from hard work grows over time. Proverbs 13:11

You shall remember the LORD your God, for it is he who gives you power to get wealth, that he may confirm his covenant that he swore to your fathers, as it is this day. Deuteronomy 8:18 ESV

Come close to God, and God will come close to you. Wash your hands, you sinners; purify your hearts, for your loyalty is divided between God and the world. James 4:8

True humility and fear of the LORD lead to riches, honor, and long life. Proverbs 22:4

Instead of shame and dishonor, you will enjoy a double share of honor. You will possess a double portion of prosperity in your land, and everlasting joy will be yours. Isaiah 61:7

Make it Personal

Which of the Scripture verses listed in this chapter gave you new insight into God's will? Are you aware of a need for change? Pour your thoughts about it out to God. Ask Him to make you and your husband like-minded on the matter. Ask Him to direct your next discussion about money with your husband.

_____

_____

_____

_____

_____

Run from sexual sin! No other sin so clearly affects the body as this one does. For sexual immorality is a sin against your own body.

---

1 Corinthians 6:18

CHAPTER 30

SEXUAL ISSUES

God, I bring to You the heartache that covers our marriage bed. The unity missing in our marriage is evident in our sexual encounters. We have hurt each other so badly. We are so out of sync. Please help us. Please heal us.

You are aware of the deep wounds in both our hearts. The devastating effects of issues like adultery, pornography, rejection, and sexual abuse are embedded in our souls. Only You can demolish these strongholds.

God, I ask You to excavate our minds and pull out any pornographic images, fantasies and traumatic memories. You planned ahead for our healing. You allowed Jesus to carry these burdens to the cross. You allowed Him to be beaten so we could be healed. By Your unlimited power and resources, our hearts can be free from the past. I place my faith in Your power to renew our minds completely.

You are the Redeemer of our past and the Author of our future love making. Help me, God, to lay down my expectations of what my husband should be and do. Help me to be sexually generous to him. Let Your Holy Spirit lead me to present my husband with the physical love he desires by Your design. You created me to be a fountain of blessing to my husband. I choose to believe You can cause him to be completely satisfied by me.

God, I ask that You help my husband recognize that I am unique. Help him to feel safe and confident enough to ask me what I enjoy. Help him to let go of ideas of perfect performances so we can be relaxed, playful and considerate of each other's limitations.

Lord, move us to take Your definition of love into every sexual encounter. With eyes of faith, I believe we can be patient, kind, and truthful with each other about our sexual inhibitions and preferences. By Your power, we can remain faithful and unoffended when one of us is tired, stressed, sick, away from home, and unavailable to meet the other's needs.

Thank You, God, for the hope of restoration.

Amen

Declaration of Faith

My faith is in God who is able to redeem our sacred sexual union.

Scripture References

We use God's mighty weapons, not worldly weapons, to knock down the strongholds of human reasoning and to destroy false arguments.
2 Corinthians 10:4

But he was pierced for our rebellion, crushed for our sins. He was beaten so we could be whole. He was whipped so we could be healed.
Isaiah 53:5

Don't copy the behavior and customs of this world, but let God transform you into a new person by changing the way you think. Then you will learn to know God's will for you, which is good and pleasing and perfect. Romans 12:2

Surely you are still our Father! Even if Abraham and Jacob would disown us, LORD, you would still be our Father. You are our Redeemer from ages past. Isaiah 63:16

For I know the plans I have for you," says the LORD. "They are plans for good and not for disaster, to give you a future and a hope.
Jeremiah 29:11

The husband should fulfill his wife's sexual needs, and the wife should fulfill her husband's needs. 1 Corinthians 7:3

Let your wife be a fountain of blessing for you. Rejoice in the wife of your youth. She is a loving deer, a graceful doe. Let her breasts satisfy you always. May you always be captivated by her love. Proverbs 5:18-19

Love is patient and kind. Love is not jealous or boastful or proud or rude. It does not demand its own way. It is not irritable, and it keeps no record of being wronged. It does not rejoice about injustice but rejoices whenever the truth wins out. Love never gives up, never loses faith, is

always hopeful, and endures through every circumstance.
1 Corinthians 13:4-7

Then if my people who are called by my name will humble themselves and pray and seek my face and turn from their wicked ways, I will hear from heaven and will forgive their sins and restore their land. 2 Chronicles 7:14

Make it Personal

Do you have unmet expectations regarding sexual intimacy with your husband? Confide in God about what you want, what is missing, and what disappoints you. Thank Him for being your personal confidant. Next, seek His wisdom. Ask the Holy Spirit to teach you how to pray about it.

_____

_____

_____

_____

_____

_____

For jealousy and
selfishness are not
God's kind of wisdom.
Such things are earthly,
unspiritual, and demonic.

James 3:15

CHAPTER 31

FRIENDSHIP WITH THE WORLD

God, please help my husband. He seems determined to do the very opposite of what Your Word instructs us to do. I am embarrassed, sad, and often in total disbelief. How do I stay with a man who disobeys You so openly? He has chosen friendship with the world and made himself Your enemy. I'm afraid of suffering the consequences of his bad choices.

He becomes hostile toward me when I confront his behavior. This hostility is also directed toward You, God. He does not welcome Your wisdom. He is blind to his sin and any responsibility for our marriage problems.

I am clinging to Your promise of mercy. You are kind to the wicked. You are His only hope. Let Your kindness lead him to repentance.

I trust that You are far more powerful than the evil masquerading as an angel of light in his life. You command armies of angels. Please send them to liberate my husband from his spiritual blindness. I firmly believe

Your power and Your mercy have no limits. I am grateful Jesus died on the cross to pay the penalty for his sins and mine.

Fill me with Your hope, God. Let Your joy and peace carry me as I wait to see the fruit of Your relentless love for my husband. Guide my prayers for Him. Fortify my faith in Your ability to overcome this evil with Your goodness at work in me and the body of Christ. By faith, I believe my husband will be strong in You, Lord. He will be filled with faith in You and act like the man You created him to be.

Amen

Declaration of Faith

I trust God is able to make my husband strong in faith and courageous in choosing righteousness.

Scripture References

You adulterers! Don't you realize that friendship with the world makes you an enemy of God? I say it again: If you want to be a friend of the world, you make yourself an enemy of God. James 4:4

For people will love only themselves and their money. They will be boastful and proud, scoffing at God, disobedient to their parents, and ungrateful. They will consider nothing sacred. They will be unloving and unforgiving; they will slander others and have no self-control. They will be cruel and hate what is good. They will betray their friends, be reckless, be puffed up with pride, and love pleasure rather than God. They will act religious, but they will reject the power that could make them godly. Stay away from people like that! 2 Timothy 3:2-5

For the sinful nature is always hostile to God. It never did obey God's laws, and it never will. Romans 8:7

But--"When God our Savior revealed his kindness and love, he saved us, not because of the righteous things we had done, but because of his mercy. He washed away our sins, giving us a new birth and new life through the Holy Spirit. Titus 3:4-5

"Love your enemies! Do good to them. Lend to them without expecting to be repaid. Then your reward from heaven will be very great, and you will truly be acting as children of the Most High, for he is kind to those who are unthankful and wicked. Luke 6:35

Don't you see how wonderfully kind, tolerant, and patient God is with you? Does this mean nothing to you? Can't you see that his kindness is intended to turn you from your sin? Romans 2:4

But I am not surprised! Even Satan disguises himself as an angel of light. 2 Corinthians 11:14

Then the angel said to me, "Shout this message for all to hear: 'This is what the LORD of Heaven's Armies says: My love for Jerusalem and Mount Zion is passionate and strong. Zechariah 1:14

I pray that from his glorious, unlimited resources he will empower you with inner strength through his Spirit. Ephesians 3:16

Praise the LORD! Give thanks to the LORD, for he is good! His faithful love endures forever. Psalm 106:1

I pray that God, the source of hope, will fill you completely with joy and peace because you trust in him. Then you will overflow with confident hope through the power of the Holy Spirit. Romans 15:13

But those who trust in the LORD will find new strength. They will soar high on wings like eagles. They will run and not grow weary. They will walk and not faint. Isaiah 40:31

Pray in the Spirit at all times and on every occasion. Stay alert and be persistent in your prayers for all believers everywhere. Ephesians 6:18

Don't let evil conquer you, but conquer evil by doing good. Romans 12:21

Be watchful, stand firm in the faith, act like men, be strong. 1 Corinthians 16:13 ESV

Make it Personal

Consider the miraculous way God interrupted Saul's life of killing Christians and transformed him completely (Acts 9). God's mighty power began working in Paul to accomplish infinitely more than seemed possible.

Study Ephesians 3:16-20 and pray it over your husband. Invite God to do in your husband what He was able to do in Paul's life.

_____

_____

_____

_____

_____

_____

MY PRAYER FOR YOUR MARRIAGE

You are a warrior. As you prayed through the previous 31 chapters, you opened the door for God to release His extraordinary power into your world. You will never be the same. God's healing Word has already changed you in beautiful ways. You are absolutely radiant in God's eyes (Psalm 34:5).

While writing this book, I've been praying for you. The Lord has so much love for you and your husband, and He has deposited a sweet measure of it in my heart. I feel like we are friends. If we were sitting together over a cup of coffee or tea, I would grab your hand and pray this over your marriage:

God, I am grateful that Your thoughts about this woman and her husband are precious and immeasurable. Thank You for supplying all they need through Christ who connects them to the unlimited riches of

Your kingdom. Thank You for being with them each day pouring out Your mercy and pursuing them with Your unfailing love and goodness.

On behalf of this couple, I speak the mighty name of Jesus and declare His power and authority over them. Every evil force working against them and their marriage must bow its knee at the name of Jesus. I thank You, Father, for the perfect blood of Jesus that redeems this husband and wife from every sin committed by them and against them.

I rejoice in Your faithfulness to allow trials and afflictions to draw them to the power of Your Word. I trust Your Word to heal and deliver them from destructive decisions and patterns of behavior. Empower them by, Your Spirit, to seek You first and pursue a life of righteousness. Thank You for blessing their obedience to You and shielding them with Your favor.

In Jesus' name, I bless this wife and her husband with extraordinary faith and faithfulness. I bless them with the true knowledge of You and Your perfect love that casts out fear. I bless them with the ability to see themselves and each other as You see them. I bless them with the desire to live in humble obedience to You all the days of their lives. I bless them with the mind of Christ and the relentless desire to follow the leadership of Your Spirit so their life together is filled with peace.

I hide this couple and their family under the shelter of Your wings. Your faithful promises are their armor and protection. May their faith in You rise up to meet Your faithfulness.

Amen

Scripture References

How precious are your thoughts about me, O God. They cannot be numbered! I can't even count them; they outnumber the grains of sand! And when I wake up, you are still with me! Psalm 139:17-18

For in Christ lives all the fullness of God in a human body. So you also are complete through your union with Christ, who is the head over every ruler and authority. Colossians 2:9-10

And this same God who takes care of me will supply all your needs from his glorious riches, which have been given to us in Christ Jesus. Philippians 4:19

Great is his faithfulness; his mercies begin afresh each morning. Lamentations 3:23

Surely your goodness and unfailing love will pursue me all the days of my life, and I will live in the house of the LORD forever. Psalm 23:6

Therefore, God elevated him to the place of highest honor and gave him the name above all other names, that at the name of Jesus every knee should bow, in heaven and on earth and under the earth, and every tongue confess that Jesus Christ is Lord, to the glory of God the Father. Philippians 2:9-11

He is so rich in kindness and grace that he purchased our freedom with the blood of his Son and forgave our sins. Ephesians 1:7

My suffering was good for me, for it taught me to pay attention to your decrees. Psalm 119:71

He sent out his word and healed them, and delivered them from their destruction. Psalm 107:20 ESV

Seek the Kingdom of God above all else, and live righteously, and he will give you everything you need. Matthew 6:3

For you bless the righteous, O LORD; you cover him with favor as with a shield. Psalm 5:12 ESV

Such love has no fear, because perfect love expels all fear. If we are afraid, it is for fear of punishment, and this shows that we have not fully experienced his perfect love. 1 John 4:18

True humility and fear of the LORD lead to riches, honor, and long life. Proverbs 22:4

For, "Who can know the LORD's thoughts? Who knows enough to teach him?" But we understand these things, for we have the mind of Christ. 1 Corinthians 2:16

So letting your sinful nature control your mind leads to death. But letting the Spirit control your mind leads to life and peace. Romans 8:6

He will cover you with his feathers. He will shelter you with his wings. His faithful promises are your armor and protection. Psalm 91:4

Join the Marriage Armor Community

Would you like to be continually encouraged in praying your marriage?

I created **Marriage Armor for the #PrayingBride**, a free email subscription offering you simple, Scriptural prayers and short devotions on how to apply God's Word to your marriage. When you subscribe, you will receive two to three emails a week as well as access to an online prayer support group.

Join me and thousands of wives who are committed to seeking God's best for their marriages. Go to **jenniferowhite.com/marriage-armor** to preview examples and register for your free subscription.

About the Author

Hi there, friend! Thanks for joining me here in this book of prayers for your marriage. It's been my joy to craft prayers for your marriage and help you see how His Word applies to your relationship with Him and your spouse.

As I write this, I've been married to David for nineteen years. We had both been in marriages that ended in divorce. Our first marriages ended in divorce and only a few years after saying "I Do" our marriage was obviously crumbling. Instead of pursuing divorce, I cried out, "Help me Jesus" without knowing if Jesus would or could help me. His help came to me in the form of Bible studies and a counselor who taught me how to live and pray in agreement with God's Word.

I am living proof that God, through His mighty power at work in people, can accomplish infinitely more than humans can ask or imagine (Ephesians 3:20). My family and personal history should disqualify me from writing to you about marriage. But God triumphs over devastation.

He is still making me new and bringing beauty from the ashes. His Word continues to heal me and deliver me from destructive thinking. The reality of His redemption allows me to wave the banner of His victorious way over you and many other women today.

For the last several years, I've given my life to blogging, writing books, speaking, as well as painting to encourage people's faith and prayers. I hope you will also read my first book, *Prayers for New Brides: Putting on God's Armor After the Wedding Dress*. In it, you will find 40 devotions, prayer prompts and faith-building exercises to equip you to fight for your marriage. Wives of every age and stage of life have found it helpful.

Stop by **JenniferOWhite.com** for more prayer inspiration and to connect with me on social media.

Another Title by Jennifer O. White

"This book truly transformed my marriage and myself."
-- Virginia L

"A book that should have been written years ago. Prayers for New Brides...is a book that must be given to each new bride."
-- Randall M

"I actually bought this book to give to my daughter-in-law, started leafing through it, and now can't put it down. Although I have been married 30+ years, the prayers and reminders in this book are surprisingly on target even for me."
-- Traci M

"This book is not only for new brides but will benefit any woman who feels defenseless in the midst of a raging battlefield. Jennifer is vulnerable and real about the war being fought and how it must be won. She shares from her personal experience and then she provides Scripture after Scripture to build you up and give you confidence. It will challenge you and free you from many wrong ideas; and by the time you put it down, you will feel you have made a new friend."
-- Rachel N.

Send a Prayer

Share hope! Encourage others with a prayer greeting card revealing what is possible with God in their lives.

Explore the *Prayerfully Speaking* cards I created with my own original art for the perfect prayer and faith-building words for someone you love. All of the cards at 5"x7" and can be framed for display.

Go to **JenniferOWhite.com/shop** to see the vivid colors, read the messages on each card, and order.

Made in the USA
Columbia, SC
05 July 2017